Child Labour & Exploitation

Series Editor: Cara Acred

Volume 268

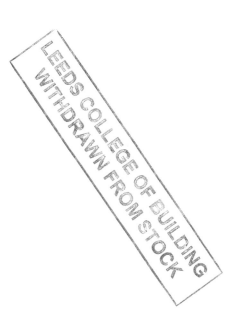

Independence Educational Publishers

First published by Independence Educational Publishers

The Studio, High Green

Great Shelford

Cambridge CB22 5EG

England

© Independence 2014

Copyright

Photocopy licence

British Library Cataloguing in Publication Data

Child labour & exploitation. -- (Issues ; 268)

1. Child labor. 2. Child sexual abuse. 3. Child soldiers.

4. Exploitation.

I. Series II. Acred, Cara editor.

331.3'1-dc23

ISBN-13: 9781861686879

Printed in Great Britain

MWL Print Group Ltd

Contents

Introduction

Child Labour & Exploitation is Volume 268 in the **ISSUES** series. The aim of the series is to offer current, diverse information about important issues in our world, from a UK perspective.

ABOUT CHILD LABOUR & EXPLOITATION

It is estimated that approximately 85 million children around the world are engaged in some form of child labour. In China alone, up to 100,000 children are employed in the manufacturing sector. This book explores the evocative topics of child labour and exploitation, looking at children's rights, child soldiers and child sexual exploitation.

OUR SOURCES

Titles in the **ISSUES** series are designed to function as educational resource books, providing a balanced overview of a specific subject.

The information in our books is comprised of facts, articles and opinions from many different sources, including:

⇨ Newspaper reports and opinion pieces

⇨ Website factsheets

⇨ Magazine and journal articles

⇨ Statistics and surveys

⇨ Government reports

⇨ Literature from special interest groups

A NOTE ON CRITICAL EVALUATION

Because the information reprinted here is from a number of different sources, readers should bear in mind the origin of the text and whether the source is likely to have a particular bias when presenting information (or when conducting their research). It is hoped that, as you read about the many aspects of the issues explored in this book, you will critically evaluate the information presented.

It is important that you decide whether you are being presented with facts or opinions. Does the writer give a biased or unbiased report? If an opinion is being expressed, do you agree with the writer? Is there potential bias to the 'facts' or statistics behind an article?

ASSIGNMENTS

In the back of this book, you will find a selection of assignments designed to help you engage with the articles you have been reading and to explore your own opinions. Some tasks will take longer than others and there is a mixture of design, writing and research-based activities that you can complete alone or in a group.

FURTHER RESEARCH

At the end of each article we have listed its source and a website that you can visit if you would like to conduct your own research. Please remember to critically evaluate any sources that you consult and consider whether the information you are viewing is accurate and unbiased.

Useful weblinks

www.amnesty.org

www.centreforsocialjustice.org.uk
(search: child)

www.childrenssociety.org.uk

www.child-soldiers.org

www.crae.org.uk

www.globalmarch.org

www.humantraffickingindicators.org

www.ilo.org

www.nspcc.org.uk

www.plan-international.org

www.soschildrensvillages.org.uk

www.un.org/news

www.unicef.org

www.worldvision.org.uk

What is child labour?

Considerable differences exist between the many kinds of work children do. Some are difficult and demanding, others are more hazardous and even morally reprehensible. Children carry out a very wide range of tasks and activities when they work.

Defining child labour

Not all work done by children should be classified as child labour that is to be targeted for elimination. Children's or adolescents' participation in work that does not affect their health and personal development or interfere with their schooling, is generally regarded as being something positive. This includes activities such as helping their parents around the home, assisting in a family business or earning pocket money outside school hours and during school holidays. These kinds of activities contribute to children's development and to the welfare of their families; they provide them with skills and experience, and help to prepare them to be productive members of society during their adult life.

The term 'child labour' is often defined as work that deprives children of their childhood, their potential and their dignity, and that is harmful to physical and mental development.

It refers to work that:

⇨ is mentally, physically, socially or morally dangerous and harmful to children; and

⇨ interferes with their schooling by:

• depriving them of the opportunity to attend school;

• obliging them to leave school prematurely; or

• requiring them to attempt to combine school attendance with excessively long and heavy work.

In its most extreme forms, child labour involves children being enslaved, separated from their families, exposed to serious hazards and illnesses and/or left to fend for themselves on the streets of large cities – often at a very early age. Whether or not particular forms of 'work' can be called 'child labour' depends on the child's age, the type and hours of work performed, the conditions under which it is performed and the objectives pursued by individual countries. The answer varies from country to country, as well as among sectors within countries.

The worst forms of child labour

Whilst child labour takes many different forms, a priority is to eliminate without delay the worst forms of child labour as defined by Article 3 of ILO Convention No. 182:

(a) all forms of slavery or practices similar to slavery, such as the sale and trafficking of children, debt bondage and serfdom and forced or compulsory labour, including forced or compulsory recruitment of children for use in armed conflict;

(b) the use, procuring or offering of a child for prostitution, for the production of pornography or for pornographic performances;

(c) the use, procuring or offering of a child for illicit activities, in particular for the production and trafficking of drugs as defined in the relevant international treaties;

(d) work which, by its nature or the circumstances in which it is carried out, is likely to harm the health, safety or morals of children.

Labour that jeopardises the physical, mental or moral well-being of a child, either because of its nature or because of the conditions in which it is carried out, is known as 'hazardous work'.

⇨ The above information is reprinted with kind permission from the International Labour Organization. Please visit www. ilo.org for further information.

© International Labour Organization 2014

How does child labour prevent literacy?

Across the world, child labour is a major factor preventing children from going to school and equipping themselves with literacy skills. Poverty forces many children into work, but being illiterate will further propel the poverty cycle. With International Literacy Day just a couple of days away, SOS Children investigates this complex problem that keeps millions of children out of school every day.

What is meant by 'child labour'?

For many, the term 'child labour' might conjure up images of sweatshops and crowded factories, which exploit young children and neglect their well-being. While this may be true in some cases, there are many other types of child labour, and some types of child work which are even considered as a positive way of developing skills. So how can we draw a line between what is acceptable child work, and what is harmful child labour?

The International Labour Organization (ILO) is the authority in defining child labour. They have considered all types of child work; from light work (such as helping with chores at home), difficult and demanding work (e.g. agricultural tasks), through to the worst forms of child labour which are hazardous and even morally reprehensible (including child prostitution). The ILO has categorised child work according to the type and hours of work performed,

the conditions under which it is performed, and the age of the child.

The ILO states that child labour is work that deprives children of their childhood, their potential and their dignity, and is harmful to physical and mental development. Child labour refers to work that:

⇨ is mentally, physically, socially or morally dangerous and harmful to children; and interferes with their schooling by:

- depriving them of the opportunity to attend school;

- obliging them to leave school prematurely; or

- requiring them to attempt to combine school attendance with excessively long and heavy work.

Child labour is a violation of a child's rights. In Article 32 of the Convention on the Rights of the Child it is declared,

'(we) recognise the right of the child to be protected from economic exploitation and from performing any work that is likely to be hazardous or to interfere with the child's education, or to be harmful to the child's health or physical, mental, spiritual, moral or social development.'

How big of a problem is child labour?

Although difficult to accurately measure, it's estimated that about 150,000,000 children (5–14 years old) are involved in child labour worldwide. If we consider all young people who are under 18, some estimates are as high as 246 million. Of these, nearly 70% work in hazardous conditions.

Child labour is a global problem. Regional estimates indicate that the largest number of child workers in the five to 14 age group are in the Asia and Pacific region, where 127.3 million children work (19%

of children in the region). In sub-Saharan Africa there is an estimated 48 million child workers – that's almost one child in three (29%) below the age of 15 who is economically active. 16% of children work in Latin America and the Caribbean – that's approximately 17.4 million children, and 15% of children in the Middle East and North Africa are working. Finally in developed and transition economies, 2.5 million and 2.4 million children are working, respectively.

Looking at the 5–17-year-olds who are child labourers, it's estimated that 60% of them work in agriculture, 26% in services and 7% in industry, with the remainder in undefined work. Although numbers show that more boys than girls are involved in child labour, this may be because many of the types of work that girls do are invisible – such as being a domestic servant. Of the children involved in domestic work, roughly 90% of children are girls.

Child labour tends to be concentrated in the informal sector of the economy (this means the part of the economy that isn't taxed, monitored by the Government or included in a country's GNP). For some work children are not paid, only receiving food and a place to sleep. Working in the informal sector is more risky as children have less protection if they suffer violence or maltreatment by their employer,

and if they become injured or ill they can be dismissed and not receive payment.

As you can see – child labour is a huge problem. Beyond these statistics, the real damage of child labour are the long-term consequences on a child's ability to attain a decent quality of life, in which they're happy and healthy. Whatever the reasons for a child working, the effects are similarly damaging. Child labour interferes with a child's physical and mental development, violates their rights, and is an obstacle to gaining basic education.

Without going to school, children labourers are unlikely to learn how to read and write, meaning they won't enjoy the vital benefits and freedoms that literacy brings. Findings from Brazil by the World Bank demonstrate that early entry into the labour force reduces lifetime earnings by some 13 to 20%, increasing significantly the probability of being poor later in life.

Why do children work?

We've looked at what child labour is – but why does it continue to exist in today's world? The answer is not straightforward, and requires looking at many interconnected factors. We need to consider both the supply side of child labour, that is, the children who are working,

as well as the demand side of child labour, meaning those who employ children.

The most compelling reason why children work is poverty. The income that a child can bring to a poor household can be vital to a family's survival. Yet poverty doesn't fully explain child labour, as countries may be equally poor but have relatively high or low levels of child labour. Other factors influencing how much child labour there is in a country includes:

Barriers to education. In many parts of the world, basic education is not available for all children, especially in remote rural areas. Where schools are available, they might not be free. Even in many countries which boast free primary education, there are often hidden costs such as buying uniforms, textbooks, and stationery, which many families simply can't afford. Furthermore, when the quality of education is poor, and the lessons not relevant, parents might not see the value in sending their child to school, and therefore going to work is preferred.

Culture and tradition. Where there are few opportunities for children even with advanced education, parents may share a cultural norm in which labour is seen as more valuable and productive. In many cultures, particularly where the informal economy is large, children are often expected to pursue their parents' trade or take over a small household business, so that training from a young age seems advantageous. Another cultural norm which exists in many cultures is that educating girls is less valuable, or not expected, and these girls may instead work, providing domestic services, for instance.

Market demand. Employers may actively prefer to hire children because they can be paid lower wages than adults, can be dispensed of easily and also form a docile, obedient work-force that will not seek to organise itself for protection and support. Another important factor to consider is that the informal economy is growing, especially in developing countries, meaning it is increasingly more attractive for employers to recruit children.

The effects of income shocks on households. Natural disasters, economic or agricultural crises or the impact of disease including HIV, AIDS, can cause a sudden loss of family income. During these unpredictable events, child labour may be resorted to as a coping mechanism. If a parent falls ill due to HIV or AIDS related illnesses, the child may have to drop out of school to care for family members. The phenomenon of child-headed households is also associated with the HIV, AIDS epidemic as orphaned children work to care for younger siblings.

Inadequate/poor enforcement of legislation and policies to protect children. Child labour persists when national laws and policies to protect children are lacking or are not effectively implemented and policed.

Discrimination and vulnerability amongst certain groups in a society. Social inequities may cause child labour, but they are also a consequence. Children who belong to discriminated sections of a community, such as from indigenous or minority groups or lower castes, are more likely to drop out of school and work. Migrant children are also vulnerable to hidden and illicit labour.

How can we eliminate child labour?

The damaging and enduring consequences of child labour demand that the problem is urgently addressed and child labour is eliminated across the world. However, the many causes of child labour, and the reasons behind it, demonstrate that any solution needs to have a multi-pronged approach. Juan Somavia, the Director-General of ILO, states that:

'No to child labour is our stance. Yet 215 million are in child labour as a matter of survival. A world without child labour is possible with the right priorities and policies: quality education, opportunities for young people, decent work for parents, a basic social protection floor for all. Driven by conscience, let's muster the courage and conviction to act in solidarity and ensure every child's right to his or her childhood. It brings rewards for all.'

To eliminate child labour is to break intergenerational cycles of poverty, strengthen national economies and make progress on achieving the Millennium Development Goals. Policies to tackle child labour need to put children's welfare at the centre, while working towards creating a protective environment. This includes the provision of good quality, accessible, relevant and free schools with basic education as compulsory. Attending school and gaining academic success needs to be seen as a better option than work – requiring shifts in cultural norms as well as an opening up of economic and social opportunities.

6 September 2013

⇨ The above information is reprinted with kind permission from SOS Children. Please visit www.soschildrensvillages.org.uk for further information.

© Rainbow Wilcox/ SOS Children 2014

'I could make six bracelets in a day': the life of a child worker

For a lot of children in the UK it's back to school after a half-term of wild weather and playing indoors! But in many developing countries, children are denied an education and forced to work as child labourers. In today's blog we hear from Sonali, a 12-year-old girl from India, who had dreams of becoming a teacher but was forced into hours of painful work making bracelets for a pittance. Through World Vision's help, Sonali is now in school and able to look forward to a future full of hope and possibilities.

By Annila Harris

Clutching a box of beads in her hand, Sonali sheepishly says, 'Come, I'll show you.'

Kneeling down, she opens the plastic container, revealing glittering plastic beads of pink, white, green and yellow. She takes a pink thread and, peeping through with one eye closed, runs it through the needle head first time with precision.

As she ties a knot at the end of the thread, she starts narrating the process of making a bracelet.

'Now take the needle and run it through the two beads of the same colour. Interlink them and create a pattern. This is how I made anklets and necklaces.'

Sonali was five years old when she made her first piece of jewellery. Turning a blind eye to education, Sonali's family kept her at home, where she assisted her mother in crafting intricate jewellery.

Her father's daily earnings of US$1.60 rarely went towards supporting his family of seven, instead more commonly being spent on alcohol, which he consumed in excessive amounts.

'My father was unable to work much, so there was not enough money in the house; that is why I had to help my mother make jewellery,' says Sonali.

Exhibiting the items she used to make, Sonali says, 'My mother taught me how to make jewellery. It took me an hour to make one bracelet. I could make six bracelets in a day but chains took more time because it needed more work. So it took me two to three days to make one necklace.'

Despite every drop of sweat poured out to craft each piece, the family only made US$1 per day. With pittance to eat, education seemed like an unnecessary investment for Sonali's father and a distant dream for Sonali.

'I did want to be playing and studying,' she says. 'I had dreams of becoming a teacher.'

An often-hidden problem

According to World Vision's community development coordinator, Chawang Shangar, occupations like embroidery work, artificial jewellery work, bamboo crafts and textile work have always been more prone to employing child labourers.

Raw materials are often delivered to homes, where the entire family participates in getting the work done. In such cases many children work from their respective homes, hidden and unidentified as child labourers by the outside world.

> 'Sonali was five years old when she made her first piece of jewellery. Turning a blind eye to education, Sonali's family kept her at home, where she assisted her mother in crafting intricate jewellery'

'Sonali was seven when we first met her. She was not going to school simply because the family did not have money to send the children to school,' says Prema, a World Vision volunteer who teaches at a transit school initiated by World Vision.

Bringing Sonali to the World Vision transit school was an uphill battle, one the volunteers were ready to face head on. The key to unlocking the doors to Sonali's house was to empower and educate her mother first.

'The volunteers explained the importance of education. They told me that if I don't educate my children they lose out on having a productive life,' Sonali's mother, Meena, recalls. 'The challenges I face because I am uneducated, they would have to face too.'

Meena decided to send Sonali and her siblings to the World Vision transit centre, where children are given basic education free of charge.

'When I first started coming to the centre I felt strange and uncomfortable,' Sonali remembers. 'I was scared. There were so many children studying in the room.'

Transformation

From no education, to part education and part work, to solely focusing on education, weaning off from labour was a gradual but certain process. Now 12, Sonali is in Grade 5.

Her transition from transit school to formal education centre was finally complete with World Vision enrolling her in the local school.

Beaming away she says, 'I love Hindi because it has reading comprehension, phrases and proverbs. We get to write paragraphs.'

Looking back at her past life, Sonali says without hesitation, 'Children should study because when they grow up they can become someone big, like a doctor, teacher. Children should not work.'

With constant support and encouragement from her mother, Sonali now sails through her everyday life never having to fear how her world would be without education. She is free to enjoy her childhood.

'From no education, to part education and part work, to solely focusing on education, weaning off from labour was a gradual but certain process. Now 12, Sonali is in Grade 5'

But it's not just Sonali who has benefitted: inspired by her daughter's courage, Meena has developed a passion for social justice. Now a confident, driven and feisty lady, she has linked herself with other local organisations to proactively fight against domestic violence and encourage women's empowerment.

'Sonali now sails through her everyday life never having to fear how her world would be without education. She is free to enjoy her childhood'

'Before, I never stepped out of my house. Being part of various meetings and awareness programmes run by World Vision gave me the confidence to speak out and not to tolerate injustice. Now I have a voice and an opinion,' Meena says.

25 February 2014

⇨ The above information is reprinted with kind permission from World Vision. Please visit www.worldvision.org.uk for further information.

India's mica mines: the shameful truth behind mineral make-up's shimmer

In the hills of Jharkhand in India, child labourers mine the mica that brings sparkle to the world.

By Ben Doherty and Sarah Whyte

Mohammed Salim Ansari is worried he is in trouble. Crouched, alone and barefoot, and carrying a sharpened stick he uses to hack at the wall of earth in front of him, he thinks we have come to take him from his family.

Frightened, almost in tears, he is mollified when we explain we only want to talk about his work, and he quietly goes back to his crude mining in a small hollow of rock.

'Heritage Brands, which owns Australis, Innoxa and Revlon, says it audits and insists on accreditation for all suppliers and does not source any products from India. But the company could not provide specific information about the "source of raw materials used by all our suppliers"'

The low hills of Jharkhand shimmer in the afternoon sun, but all that glitters is not gold. The precious mineral lode of these mountains, in India's poor, remote east, does not bring riches to those who mine it. Instead, the mica that gives sparkle to the world means only grinding work, and an unremitting, unprofitable obligation to do more of it.

Mica is a mineral coveted for centuries for its unique lustre. But its myriad uses in modern products now make it a valuable commodity. It is mica that gives make-up products such as eyeshadow, nail polish, lipstick and concealer their shimmer.

Mica gives automotive paints their shine, is used in building materials, and as an insulator in electronic chips. It is found in lasers and radar.

This impoverished district has the largest known mica deposits in the world. The mineral here is easily accessible, high quality and in demand from all corners of the globe.

But the industry here is little better than a black market, dependent on a huge unskilled workforce, forced into working for lower and lower prices. Profits are made off the backs of children.

Salim, 12, has been mining for a year, he says, helping out his father who is further down the hill. He insists he goes to school every day and only mines when he comes home. We find him shortly after 1pm, and when we ask him what his teacher's name is he says he doesn't know.

Others in the village say that he enrolled in school, but doesn't go. He mines every day.

'I don't like this,' he says, as he hacks at the rock. The cracked plastic tray he fills with mica flakes can carry a kilogram. He will fill it ten times today. Each kilogram earns him five rupees, about 8¢. Depending on its quality and type, mica on the international market can fetch anywhere from several dollars a kilogram to more than $1,000.

But the 50 rupees Salim earns each day is a vital adjunct to his parents' income. They need him to work, he explains, 'to help earn money'.

The work is hard and dangerous. Children working risk snake and scorpion bites, and the hollowed-out caves they mine in often collapse. They suffer cuts and skin infections, as well as respiratory illnesses, such as bronchitis, silicosis and asthma.

But however difficult and dangerous, Salim's work, officially at least, doesn't exist.

India officially produces about 15,000 tonnes of crude and scrap mica a year, according to the Government's Bureau of Mines. It has a few hundred tonnes stockpiled.

Yet it exported more than 130,000 tonnes – more than eight times the official production figure – in 2011–12, more than half of it to China.

'At present, the majority of mica mining and trade is illegal,' India's industry secretary A.P. Singh drily notes of the massive discrepancy.

The bulk of India's exports of high-quality mica flakes come from illegal mines like this one, and much of it from the work of child miners such as Salim. But where the truckloads of mica are going, and for what purpose, is deliberately kept hidden by the suppliers who are at the beginning of a complex and clandestine supply chain.

In Australia and around the world, mica remains one of the key ingredients used in the make-up and nail polish put on faces and fingers every day. It's an ingredient used not only to add shine to the make-up but to absorb excess oils and give it a consistent texture. The mineral can also be called Glimmer, Kaliglimmer, Muskovit, or may only be named by the code CI 77019.

Australian cosmetics brand Napoleon Perdis lists mica as a primary ingredient in many of its products, including its 'Prismatic Eyeshadow', 'DeVine Goddess Lipstick' and its 'Auto Pilot' skin primer, priced between $30 and $52.

After months of e-mails from Fairfax Media, the company would not disclose where the mica used in its products is sourced from, or who the company's suppliers are.

'As we are a private company, we wouldn't be able to provide our actual supplier name,' a Napoleon Perdis spokeswoman says.

Estée Lauder Companies, which owns exclusive brands MAC, Clinique, Bobbi Brown and its own line Estée Lauder, says it sources less than ten per cent of its mica from India, but is working with a local community organisation to eliminate child labour.

'The Estée Lauder Companies are aware of the complexities surrounding mica sourcing in India, and recognise the need for practical solutions to the complex socio-economic challenges within sourcing communities,' a spokeswoman says. 'Since 2006, we have partnered with local NGO, Bachpan Bachao Andolan (BBA), to promote access to education as an approach to work towards the elimination of child labour in mica-sourcing communities.'

Heritage Brands, which owns Australis, Innoxa and Revlon, says it audits and insists on accreditation for all suppliers and does not source any products from India. But the company could not provide specific information about the 'source of raw materials used by all our suppliers'.

'We do not believe that any of our products are associated with child labour,' a spokeswoman says. 'All of our manufacturers are accredited with their social and ethical responsibility for their quality assurance and factory standards.'

Make-up giant L'Oréal Group, which owns brands including Lancome, L'Oréal, Maybelline, Redken, The Body Shop and Yves Saint Laurent, did not reply to the questions sent by Fairfax.

Products such as Maybelline's Mineral Powder Finishing Veil Translucent Loose Powder lists '100 per cent mica-minerals' on its packaging while many of Lancome's products, including its blush, eyeshadow and mascara, say they 'may contain' mica on their ingredients list.

Mica used in cosmetics has been linked to child labour in the past. In 2009, German pharmaceutical and chemicals company Merck KGaA, which supplies mica to cosmetics brands around the world, including S. Black in London, was accused of using children to mine mica in India.

The pharmaceutical giant says that since 2011 it has implemented a 'mica tracking system' and a 'two-pronged approach' to ensure it has full control of its supply chain. 'Therefore, we are able to guarantee that no children are involved in mica sourcing and

processing,' spokesman Gerhard Lerch says.

Back in Jharkhand, Salim's village will sell its mica to small traders, who will consolidate several villages' work to sell on to bigger suppliers, who sell it on to exporters and – usually through China – to the world's cosmetics houses, paint companies and electronics manufacturers.

'Mohammed Salim Ansari is worried he is in trouble. Crouched, alone and barefoot, and carrying a sharpened stick he uses to hack at the wall of earth in front of him, he thinks we have come to take him from his family'

That child labour is used in India's mica mining is known. Commissioner with the Indian Government's National Commission for Protection of Child Rights Yogesh Dube recently visited Jharkhand: 'Child labour and trafficking are major issues in Jharkhand and it is high time that people understand that,' he says.

Two decades ago, in the face of environmental concerns and in an effort to better regulate the mica industry, the Government shut mines across the state. But the closures have driven child labour further, literally and metaphorically, underground.

The industry is intentionally kept arcane, says Kailash Satyarthi, founder of child rights organisation Bachpan Bachao Andolan.

Those who work at the mine are unaware of where their product ultimately ends up, and those who buy the mica are wilfully blind to where it comes from.

'It is like a mafia – there is a black market for this, there are subcontractors in each village who rely on these children's labour. But the miners don't know where the mica they mine ends up. They are the third, fourth, fifth

layer in the supply chain, and the subcontractors and the suppliers deliberately don't tell them where it goes.'

BBA has helped create 'child-friendly villages' across Jharkhand, where children do not work. It has established schools for primary school-aged children in those villages and provides bicycles to older students so they can travel to nearby secondary schools. In communities where children are expected to be in school, rather than at work, attendance rates are above 90 per cent.

Industry efforts at reform, however, have been ineffective. India has strong child labour laws, which prohibit anyone under 18 working in mining, but enforcement is lax, where it exists at all.

'Products such as Maybelline's Mineral Powder Finishing Veil Translucent Loose Powder lists "100 per cent mica-minerals" on its packaging while many of Lancome's products, including its blush, eyeshadow and mascara, say they "may contain" mica on their ingredients list'

'The situation is not easy in that area,' Satyarthi says. 'The Naxalites [a Maoist rebel army] control the jungle, police are regularly killed, and government officials cannot go there, so there is no control.'

The day before Fairfax Media visits this mine site, two police were ambushed on a nearby road. They were decapitated and their heads left in the road as a warning.

In the nearby town of Jhumri Telaiya, whole streets are dedicated to the mica trade, most of it black market. Men in kurta pyjamas sit in front of enormous sacks full of mica flakes for export.

Trader Rajesh Jain says government closures of legal mines have simply forced people into working illegally. 'The illegal mining continues. Hundreds of thousands of villages are involved in this trade. They are dependent on it, and they are very poor. Without this they would have no income at all.'

Jain won't reveal to whom he supplies mica, but says the government should grant more mining licences so the industry here can be properly policed.

'In all of India, only Jharkhand has the high-quality mica, the quality for the cosmetics industry, so the demand is strong. 90 per cent of the mica mined in Jharkhand goes overseas; electronics, paints, automobiles and cosmetics industries are the major buyers.'

Fairfax visits and is briefly allowed access to a legal mine, but armed security guards quickly surround us and insist we leave.

A group of women is at lunch, sitting under a tree. Two of the group look especially young, about ten or 11 years old, but we are forbidden from speaking with them or taking photographs.

Outside the gates of the mine, the dense jungle is scarred with the ad hoc mines, and the discarded red tailings that spill down the hills.

Beside a nearby road, 12-year-old Renu and ten-year-old Khushbu, migrant girls from the same village, are crouched in a pit, filling plastic tubs like Salim's.

The sun above them is fierce, and the entire landscape shimmers with the piles of mica waiting for sale.

Renu says the work is hard. It cuts her hands and makes her unwell. 'I don't like it, but my family are here.'

Talo Singh, a relative, says both girls have been working in this mine for about four months. 'Our family migrated here for work, so there is nothing wrong if our entire family works for our livelihood,' he says in explanation as to why the girls don't go to school.

Khushbu, who looks even younger than her age as she expertly gathers the shiny mica flakes, says

'Two decades ago, in the face of environmental concerns and in an effort to better regulate the mica industry, the Government shut mines across the state. But the closures have driven child labour further, literally and metaphorically, underground'

she knows about make-up, and that the mica she mines each day ends up as decoration on the faces of women overseas.

'It is used in powder for ladies.'

19 January 2014

⇨ The above information is reprinted with kind permission from Ben Doherty, Sarah Whyte/Fairfax Syndication. Please visit www.theage.com.au for further information.

Child Labour Index 2014

South America leads battle against child labour but Russia and China are lagging.

Two of the world's largest growth markets, Russia and China, have shown significant increases in child labour risks over the last year, reveals the latest Child Labour Index from Maplecroft. This exposes companies with operations and supply chains in these countries to greater risks of reputational and legal damage from complicity with children's rights violations.

According to Maplecroft, significant increases in child labour risks are visible in only a few countries. China dropped from the 53rd highest risk geography to 20th in the Index, while Russia fell 11 places to 69th. Both are classified as posing an 'extreme risk'. Substantial negative changes to the risk profiles of Nepal (14th, 34th in 2013), Guinea (30th, 36th in 2013), and Equatorial Guinea (109th, 114th in 2013) were also noted.

Maplecroft's ranking of 197 countries includes 83 countries rated 'extreme risk', with Eritrea, Somalia, DR Congo, Myanmar, Sudan, Afghanistan, Pakistan, Zimbabwe, Yemen and Burundi comprising the ten countries where the problem of child labour is greatest. Although none of these countries have shown significant improvement over the past year, Myanmar has moved from its position of first (as the worst performing country worldwide) in all six previous editions of the Child Labour Index, to third in the 2014 Index. This reflects improving government commitments and capacities to combat child labour. However, the situation remains grave. For example, children are recruited as child soldiers by military and rebel groups to perform non-combatant tasks. In addition, children from Myanmar are increasingly vulnerable to unsafe migration and trafficking for labour exploitation, both within the country and cross border.

The Child Labour Index 2014 evaluates the frequency and severity of reported child labour incidents, as well as the performance of governments in preventing child labour and ensuring the accountability of perpetrators. It has been developed to enable companies to understand and identify risks of children being employed within their supply chains in violation of international standards on minimum age of employment or in

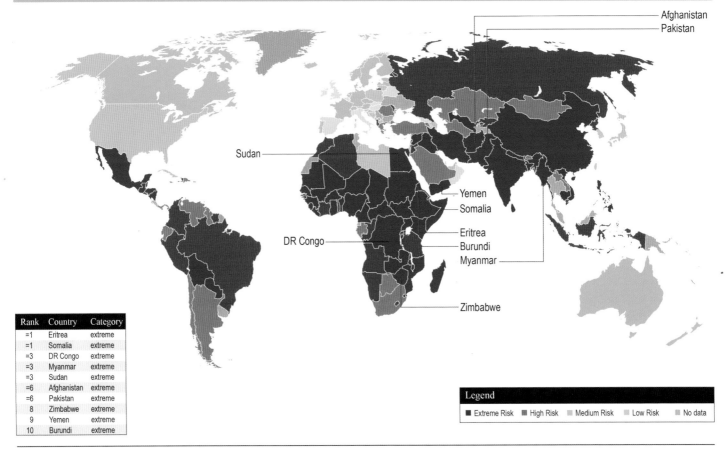

Child Labour Index 2014

maplecroft
risk responsibility reputation

Rank	Country	Category
=1	Eritrea	extreme
=1	Somalia	extreme
=3	DR Congo	extreme
=3	Myanmar	extreme
=3	Sudan	extreme
=6	Afghanistan	extreme
=6	Pakistan	extreme
8	Zimbabwe	extreme
9	Yemen	extreme
10	Burundi	extreme

Legend

■ Extreme Risk ■ High Risk ▨ Medium Risk ▨ Low Risk □ No data

© Maplecroft 2013 | The Towers, St Stephen's Road, Bath BA1 5JZ, United Kingdom | t: +44 (0) 1225 420 000 | www.maplecroft.com | info@maplecroft.com

occupations that limit or damage their overall development.

Global trafficking is an enabler of child labour – with migrant children the most vulnerable group. The problem is particularly prevalent in China and Russia, both of which have been downgraded by the US Department of State from Tier 2 Watch List to Tier 3 in its *Trafficking in Persons Report 2013*. This is due to the Government's ongoing failure to comply with minimum standards, or make significant efforts to do so.

Trafficking is a critical factor in Russia's increasing risk profile in the Child Labour Index. Inefficient law enforcement, weak institutional capacity and corruption are important contributing factors. The last ten to 12 years have seen significant changes in the nature of child labour in Russia, especially among migrant children who, increasingly, are found working in shops and on construction sites. Children performing work in Russia are also often engaged in the worst forms of child labour, especially in rural areas where agricultural work may involve risks to their health, such as using dangerous machinery and harmful pesticides.

A climate of impunity endures in China due to the poor enforcement of child labour laws, exacerbated by a significant internal migrant population. Official statistics are not available, but estimates suggest that up to 100,000 children are employed in the manufacturing sector alone. The use of child labour in vocational 'work and study' schemes, as well as the continued employment of children in factories, present significant supply chain risks to companies even in the most economically-developed provinces.

Maplecroft's analysis indicates that child labour risks are also increasing in sub-Saharan Africa, which hosts 43 (over 50%) of the 'extreme risk' countries in the Child Labour Index.

'Africa is a significant location for foreign direct investment and has compelling growth potential,' states Lizabeth Campbell, Head of Human Rights and Societal Risk at Maplecroft. 'Despite this, child labour risks are increasing in some regions of East and West Africa, such as Tanzania and Kenya in the East and Ghana and Mali in the West. This increase is due to industrial growth in a context of inadequate labour inspections, and, in some instances, a persistent lack of human security. This reinforces the need for stringent human rights due diligence programmes in both company operations and supply chains.'

However, there are signs of an improving global outlook. In September 2013, the International Labour Organization (ILO) estimated that the rate of 5–17-year-olds engaged in child labour has decreased globally from 13.6 per cent in 2008 to 10.6 per cent in 2012. The number of children involved in the worst forms of child labour has also decreased from 115 million to 85 million during this time.

Maplecroft's findings also reveal significant improvements in addressing child labour for certain growth economies. South America is the most improved region, and has been downgraded from 'extreme' to 'high risk' in the Child Labour Index. Strong progress in Colombia (72nd, 35th in 2013) and Brazil (81st, 65th in 2013) is a key factor contributing to this improving risk profile. Since last year, the countries climbed 37 and 16 places in the rankings, respectively. This improvement is partially due to the implementation of financial aid programmes to lift poor families out of poverty, which is a principal cause of child labour. Child labour risks may, however, spike in the lead up to the 2014 World Cup in Brazil due to the employment of children in the construction of infrastructure projects related to the event.

⇨ The above information is reprinted with kind permission from Maplecroft. Please visit www.maplecroft.com for further information.

Child labour will end only if businesses respect children's rights

How can business help move children from the supply chain into the classroom? Georg Kell calls for companies to improve their support of the UN's Children's Rights and Business Principles.

A year and a half remains before the deadline for the Millennium Development Goals (MDGs) expires. Some goals have been achieved – targets on poverty reduction and access to fresh water were met in 2010, for instance, five years ahead of schedule.

Other goals are not on track. Universal primary school enrolment is one of them. There are various reasons why this ambitious dream has not been realised, and one of the main ones is the prevalence of child labour.

According to the Centre for Understanding Children's Work (UCW), one in four children not in school find themselves outside the classroom because they are enrolled at a workplace instead.

It is often said that the tragedy of such practices is that they rob children of 'a proper childhood'. But taking children off the educational track early, and sometimes irretrievably, also denies them a proper adulthood. Meanwhile, society is denied the kinds of workers, entrepreneurs and public leaders it needs to meet the challenges of the 21st century.

As the MDG deadlines approach, and having just marked the first anniversary of the launch of the Children's Rights and Business Principles for business, I have joined with Gordon Brown and ILO director-general Guy Ryder in sending a letter to more than 7,000 firms from regions around the world that are participating in the UN Global Compact, urging them to improve their support for these principles.

To eliminate child labour, we need careful effort from businesses on the ground. Dropping operations that utilise underage workers from a supply chain does not always stop them from finding other outlets. Removing child workers abruptly from their jobs can have the unintended consequence of depriving poor households of a source of income, leaving the children at risk of even more serious exploitation without necessarily ensuring that they end up in school.

A multi-dimensional, multi-stakeholder, collaborative approach seems to be what works best. In the Indian carpet-producing region of Uttar Pradesh, for example, Ikea supports suppliers in taking corrective action if child labour is identified in the chain. This approach is based on the idea that any response should not merely move child workers from one supplier's workplace to another, but should enable viable and sustainable alternatives. Working with UNICEF and child rights organisations, the company helps to mobilise communities around better schools and higher enrolment.

Crucially, the approach also involves women by improving their access to credit and income-generating opportunities and helping them to act as advocates for child rights.

Our letter to businesses states: 'When children have access to quality education, child labour prevalence is greatly reduced and economic and social development is promoted.' This is a commonsense approach. Parents who see no educational opportunities for their children have less motivation to withdraw them from work situations and less reason to hope that something better awaits their daughters and sons.

Despite strong progress on the MDG of universal primary school enrolment, the most recent UN statistics show that 10% of children in the developing world still are out of school. In Africa, the proportion is close to one quarter, and many of those who are in school are studying in one-room buildings without electricity, books, bathroom facilities or any separation between grades.

The International Cocoa Initiative (ICI), which represents various trade associations, individual companies and civil society organisations, is raising awareness of the problem of child labour in West Africa and supporting communities to build and equip new schools. It is reported that school enrolment rose in ICI communities in 2007–11, by 16% in Ivory Coast and by 24% in Ghana.

Agriculture is a particularly important front in the battle against child labour practices. According to the ILO, farm work is the occupation in which around 60% of underage labourers are engaged.

This is not surprising since extreme poverty is most intensive and schools least prevalent, in the rural regions of the developing world. Most farmers in poor countries have a tenuous legal hold on small parcels of land, either trying to feed themselves or feed into agricultural supply chains. It is not surprising that children are caught up in the desperate effort to achieve subsistence. Together with a renewed drive to improve schooling, steps to upgrade agricultural production in the developing world are key to the eradication of child labour practices.

Our letter encourages companies to invest in education, to publicly identify their actions in support of children's rights and to engage in new commitments to secure our common future, which is our children.

18 April 2013

⇨ The above information is reprinted with kind permission from *The Guardian*. Please visit www.theguardian.com for further information.

Children and human rights

Across the world children are denied their human rights, including for example, their right to education. They are recruited into armed forces. They are subjected to the death penalty, are disappeared, are punished by cruel and inhumane methods and suffer many other forms of violence.

Child soldiers

Worldwide, hundreds of thousands of children under 18 have been affected by armed conflict.

They are recruited into government armed forces, paramilitaries, civil militia and a variety of other armed groups. Often they are abducted at school, on the streets or at home. Others enlist 'voluntarily', usually because they see few alternatives. Yet international law prohibits the participation in armed conflict of children aged under 18.

It means that in reality girls and boys illegally and under force, participate in combat where frequently they are injured or killed. Others are used as spies, messengers, porters, servants or to lay or clear landmines. Girls are at particular risk of rape and other sexual abuse.

Such children are robbed of their childhood and exposed to terrible dangers and to psychological and physical suffering.

Other forms of violence against children

Children routinely face other violence – at school, in institutions meant for their protection, in juvenile detention centres and too often in their own homes.

Violence against children happens in all parts of the world.

A small – and diminishing – number of countries execute those who were children at the time of their offences. Since 2004, only China, Iran, Pakistan and Sudan have put child offenders to death. Ending the execution of child offenders is a major objective in itself and an important step on the road to total abolition of the death penalty.

The right to education

Everyone has the right to education – which should be available free to all at least at the primary level. Education is also indispensable in realising other human rights.

Across the world many children miss out on their education because:

⇨ they are made to work

⇨ they are recruited into armed forces

⇨ their families do not have the means to pay for schooling

⇨ discrimination and racism undermine their chance to receive an education

⇨ they face violence as they pursue their education.

School fees and related costs are a common barrier to education. These charges – which may be called 'voluntary' quotas, matriculation fees or examination costs – are a greater burden for children from poor families, and they disproportionately affect those who are racial and ethnic minorities, members of Indigenous communities and migrants.

Girls are more likely to be excluded from school than boys when there isn't enough money to go round.

Key facts

The United Nations Convention on the Rights of the Child, adopted in 1989 to protect the rights of children, is the most widely ratified human rights treaty in history. It encompasses civil rights and freedoms, family environment, basic health and welfare, education, leisure and cultural activities and special protection measures for children.

There are estimated to be between 100 million and 150 million street children in the world, and this number is growing. Of those some 5–10% have run away from or been abandoned by their families.

Under international law, the participation of children under 18 in armed conflict is generally prohibited, and the recruitment and use of children under 15 is a war crime.

Around 4,500 children are currently in detention in Pakistan. More than 3,000 of them have not been convicted of any offence; their trials have either still yet to start or have not yet been completed.

Examples of what Amnesty International is doing

As a member of the Coalition to Stop the Use of Child Soldiers, Amnesty International works to end the recruitment of children into armed forces and to reintegrate former child soldiers back into civilian life.

Amnesty International has recommended that Bosnia and Herzegovina, Croatia and Slovenia take immediate action to prohibit discrimination against Roma in education, and take further steps towards eliminating discrimination against Romani children and promoting equality in education.

Around the world, Amnesty International members, including its Youth and Student network, are campaigning to prevent the unnecessary imprisonment of children in Pakistan.

Success story

On 25 May 2000, the UN General Assembly adopted the Optional Protocol to the Convention on the Rights of the Child on the involvement of children in armed conflict. This represented a milestone in protecting children from participation in armed conflicts.

To mark the sixth anniversary of the Protocol's adoption, Amnesty International, together with the Coalition to Stop the Use of Child Soldiers, called on the Russian Federation to ratify it without any further delay and set 18 years as the standard minimum age for voluntary recruitment into its armed forces. At the time, both Russia and China were the two remaining members of the UN Security Council not to have become party to the Protocol.

Both countries subsequently ratified the document in 2008 and – as of February 2014 – a total of 152 countries are party to the Protocol with a further 20 signatories from across the UN set to enact it into law.

February 2014

⇨ The above information is reprinted with kind permission from Amnesty International. Please visit www.amnesty.org for further information.

Children can now seek justice through the UN

States urged to ratify new treaty so more children can access international justice for rights abuses.

Children whose human rights have been violated will finally be able to bring their cases to the United Nations after a new international treaty was enacted today.

Children suffer human rights abuses all over the world, including being sentenced to death, trafficked into hazardous child labour, and subjected to violence and sexual abuse. They are routinely neglected by decision makers and their views and opinions ignored. Ratify OP3 CRC, an international coalition of children's rights NGOs, says the UN will now be better equipped to address future violations of children's rights, and more pressure will be put on countries to ensure children's rights are respected.

Seeking justice

Until today, and despite its near universal ratification (all countries have ratified except Somalia, South Sudan and the United States), the UN Convention on the Rights of the Child was the only international human rights treaty that had no mechanism for victims to seek justice internationally when they could not get redress for violations of their rights nationally.

Campaigners are urging governments around the world to ratify the new treaty so more children can access justice at the UN. A state is not bound by the treaty until it ratifies it.

Ratification call

Flore-Anne Bourgeois, from Plan International and Co-Chair of Ratify OP3 CRC said: 'Children suffer violations of their rights every day through armed conflicts, discrimination, violence in their communities, schools and homes, as well as lack of access to basic services such as education and healthcare, and their views and opinions are systematically ignored. The list is long. It is about time that abuses of children's rights can be brought to the UN.'

'We urge all states to show their commitment to promoting and protecting children's rights by ratifying this new treaty without delay so more children can access international justice.'

Violation cases

The new treaty, known as the Optional Protocol to the Convention on the Rights of the Child on a Communications Procedure (OP3 CRC) was adopted by the United Nations General Assembly in December 2011. The treaty will become active in three months' time after Costa Rica ratified it today. Albania, Bolivia, Gabon, Germany, Montenegro, Portugal, Slovakia, Spain and Thailand previously ratified.

> **'Children suffer human rights abuses all over the world, including being sentenced to death, trafficked into hazardous child labour, and subjected to violence and sexual abuse'**

Cases brought under this new communications procedure will be heard by the Committee on the Rights of the Child, the UN body of 18 independent experts responsible for ensuring the implementation of the Convention on the Rights of the Child. From 14 April 2014 (three months from today), victims of all new or ongoing violations in states who have ratified the treaty can start bringing cases to the Committee if no solution is found nationally. The treaty does not cover past violations.

14 January 2014

⇨ The above information is reprinted with kind permission from Plan. Please visit www.plan-international.org for further information.

Let boys wear skirts to school, says children adviser Tam Baillie

Boys should be allowed to wear skirts to school to avoid 'serious distress' caused by gender-specific uniforms, a children's tsar has argued.

Tam Baillie, Scotland's commissioner for children and young people, suggested forcing children to wear such skirts or trousers depending on their gender could contravene laws set out by the UN Convention on the Rights of the Child.

Baillie's announcement was prompted as he stepped in to defend 13-year-old Luca Scarabello, from Falkirk.

The teenager is the latest schoolboy to raise the issue of boys wearing trousers to school, after Chris Whitehead was nominated for a human rights award after wearing a skirt to school.

But rather than proposing a blanket ban, Baillie proposed a flexible approach and encouraged further debate on the issue.

'I would agree gender-specific uniforms or dress codes can cause serious distress in gender-variant pupils. School uniforms and dress codes should not discriminate directly or indirectly against any of these protected groups.

'Schools should review their uniform code policies to ensure they do not have the effect of unlawfully discriminating against pupils with a protected characteristic.'

But Norman Wells, of the Family Education Trust, told the *Daily Telegraph*: 'This is yet another case of the language of children's rights being used in an attempt to add weight to what is nothing more than a personal minority view.'

The Convention on the Rights of the Child was established in 1989 and sets out human rights for children in 54 articles.

Article 2 (non-discrimination) states: 'It doesn't matter whether they are boys or girls ... no child should be treated unfairly on any basis' while Article 3 (best interests of the child) says: 'The best interests of children must be the primary concern in making decisions that may affect them. This particularly applies to budget, policy and law makers.'

The protection of rights of children is laid out in Article 4: 'Governments have a responsibility to take all available measures to make sure children's rights are respected, protected and fulfilled.'

All three articles could be used in Baillie's argument to ban gender-specific uniforms.

13 February 2012

⇨ The above information is reprinted with kind permission from The Huffington Post UK. Please visit www.huffingtonpost.co.uk for further information.

State of children's rights in England

Review of the Government action on United Nations' recommendations for strengthening children's rights in the UK.

Overview

In seeking membership of the UN's Human Rights Council this year, the UK Government asserted that it is 'committed to a strong, effective international human rights system'. It also claimed to be 'a passionate, committed and effective defender of human rights'.[1]

Such explicit commitment is very welcome. But over the last year, the Government has often given the impression it has no such commitment when the international and European human rights systems impact on the UK.

The UK's human rights record has been scrutinised this year by two UN Treaty Bodies: the Committee against Torture and the Committee on the Elimination of Discrimination against Women. Both condemned the UK for consistently failing to address many previously identified violations of human rights – among them rights specific to children, including the unlawful use of restraint on children in detention, the low age of criminal responsibility and the persisting legality of corporal punishment.

Next year, children's rights move to centre stage. The Government must report to the Committee on the Rights of the Child on how it has implemented the UN Convention on the Rights of the Child (UNCRC). The Government's draft report has just (October 2013) been published for consultation, and while it provides descriptions of policy changes affecting children, it contains almost no analysis of the impact these changes have had on children themselves.

Had this information been provided, the picture would be bleak. Our 2013 report shows that economic pressures have been used to justify not only a serious erosion of children's economic and social rights, such as health, food and the right to play, but also fundamental changes to our justice system. Huge cuts to legal aid and restrictions on judicial review seriously undermine children's ability to challenge rights violations across the board.

Children and their representatives must be able to seek the courts' protection when, for example, they are hungry or homeless, denied education or contact with their family or are unlawfully assaulted, mistreated or neglected. As Lord Neuberger has said: 'rights are valueless if they cannot be realised, and such realisation inevitably carries with it access to the courts'. But ensuring effective access to the courts is also a preventive measure, making it less likely that children's rights will be breached in the first place.

Using the courts to enforce children's rights should be a measure of last resort. The effective protection and implementation of children's rights relies in the first instance on key public services – social care, education, health – being accountable within the administrative system. But our report finds that this form of accountability has also been weakened by recent changes, for example in the schools system and health service. It has become increasingly difficult to identify which body is responsible for a children's rights violation, what measures are available to hold them accountable – and even to obtain the data on how children are being treated.

Summarised below are a few welcome improvements to children's rights and the most serious violations that are described in detail in the report. But perhaps the most urgent question for CRAE and other advocates of children's human rights is how can children secure their right to challenge and gain effective remedies for these violations?

General measures of implementation

The Government's very welcome 2010 commitment to have regard to children's rights when developing law and policy affecting children does not appear to have occurred in practice.

The role of the Children's Commissioner has been reformed with significant improvements in relation to children's rights. There are still concerns about the Commissioner's independence.

General principles

There is huge inequality in children's enjoyment of the right to life. The figures still show that infant mortality varies significantly according to socio-economic group; for example, babies with fathers employed as shelf stackers or care assistants ('semi-routine occupations') were almost twice as likely to die as those born to professionals.

Civil rights and freedoms

While the focus has been on the effects of austerity on children, children have also suffered incursions into their civil rights. For example:

⇨ The new system for regulating anti-social behaviour will allow children as young as ten to be issued with IPNAs (the new ASBOs) for conduct 'capable of causing nuisance and annoyance'. From 14, they can be imprisoned for breach. Children who live in social housing will be evicted if they, or a member of their family, breach an order; and

⇨ Tasers were used on children 323 times in 2011 compared with 135 times in 2009.

Family life and alternative care

Families have been placed under increasing pressure as a result of welfare reform and tax changes combined with the rising cost of living and stagnating wages. At the same time, children are failing to receive essential state support because of cuts to services.

Scandals this year exposed the scale of child abuse and exploitation, the fact that children are not listened to and taken seriously, and not well-served by the justice system. These have prompted initiatives to ensure that effective measures are taken when children report abuse, and to improve court processes so that children are not further abused by the judicial and safeguarding systems.

This Government has concentrated significant effort on facilitating adoption for looked after children, raising fears that other successful options for the long-term care of such children – such as kinship care and long-term foster placements – will be neglected.

Although successive governments including the present one, have increased support for children in the care system, outcomes for looked-after children remain dispiritingly poor. For example,

⇨ 34% of 19-year-old care-leavers were not in education, employment or training (NEET), compared to the national average for 18-year-olds of 14%.

⇨ 86% of children in care think it is important to keep siblings together, but 63% of children in the care system, whose siblings are also in care are separated from them.

Children with one or both parents in prison are three times as likely to suffer from mental health problems as other children and 44% say they need help dealing with their feelings.

Basic health and welfare

Health and welfare is dominated by the rising level of child poverty. Cuts to welfare support and tax credits combined with rising prices and low wages have led to both children living in working families and to families out of work experiencing severe deprivation, despite the Government's aim of 'making work pay'.

The impact of legislative changes intended to tackle health inequalities is yet to be seen, but there is widespread concern that the marketisation and lack of accountability within the health service will have a detrimental effect on children's health and widen inequality in access and outcomes. Services which are essential to safeguarding children's health are already being scaled back.

The report documents that:

⇨ 300,000 more children are now living in absolute low income (an increase of two per cent from last year);

⇨ Four out of five teachers report that some of their children are arriving at school hungry;

⇨ Poor children are now four times more likely to be unhealthy than richer children;

⇨ Children in the poorest households are three times more likely to have a mental illness than children in the best off households; and

⇨ 27% of births in England take place in baby-friendly hospitals, compared with 81% in Scotland, 67% in Wales and 58% in Northern Ireland.

Education, leisure and cultural activities

Inequality in education in terms of access, exclusions, outcomes, and quality of experience remains at staggering levels:

⇨ Only 66% of poor children, 43% of children with SEN, 76% of BME children and 50% of looked-after children achieved the expected level in English and mathematics at Key Stage 2, compared to the national average of 79%.

⇨ Only 36.3% of poor pupils, 22.4% of pupils with SEN and 15% of looked after children achieved 5+ A*–C at GCSE or equivalent including English and mathematics, compared to the national average of 58.8%.

⇨ Pupils with SEN (but no statement) are 11 times more likely to receive a permanent exclusion than pupils with no SEN. Poor children are four times more likely to receive a permanent exclusion than other pupils.

⇨ 22.4% of children are bullied daily, with disabled children and children from sexual minorities most at risk of bullying.

Inequality has been reducing for some groups, yet serious concern has been expressed that recently gained benefits may be lost with the diversification of the educational landscape.

Special measures of protection

Children who are particularly vulnerable to abuse have seen the most serious attacks on their rights.

Migrant and asylum-seeking children are disadvantaged in all areas. The Immigration Bill undermines their right to family life, health, housing, and to be protected from harm and to have their best interests taken into account. Failure to increase the rate of asylum support, already inadequate to meet children's basic needs, will leave then in worsening destitution. Discriminatory proposals in relation to legal aid will leave them unable to challenge most breaches of their rights.

One of the most positive findings in the report is that far fewer children are in custody than this time last year. However, inequality in the system is increasing and children continue to suffer serious abuses of their rights in detention. For example:

- The proportion of incarcerated children who are from black and minority ethnic communities has grown from 36% of children last year to 38% this year.

- Self-harm by children in the secure estate rose by 21%; and

- Restraint of children in custody rose by 17%, with numbers of children hospitalised as a result also increasing.

Disabled children have seen their right to an inclusive education undermined by the provisions in the Children and Families Bill, and have been disproportionately affected by changes to welfare, tax and service provision.

Summary of progress

- Significant progress made in relation to 30 recommendations.

- Significant deterioration in relation to 46 recommendations.

- No significant change in relation to 42 recommendations.

Reference

1. Foreign and Commonwealth Office (2013) UN Human Rights Council UNITED KINGDOM 2014–2016 Candidate

December 2013

- The above information is reprinted with kind permission from Children's Rights Alliance for England (CRAE). Please visit www.crae.org.uk for further information.

Every child counts

Revealing disparities, advancing children's rights.

Pick a country, any country. What proportion of births is registered, and how many children are thus granted an official identity and the rights that flow from it – rights to services, protection, the exercise of citizenship?

How many children die within a year of being born, and how many never live to see their fifth birthday? How long can those who do survive expect to live? Are they receiving essential vaccines and medicines to protect them against the diseases that prey on the young and vulnerable? Are they getting the nourishment they need for their bodies and minds to thrive? Do they have clean water for drinking and washing, and access to safe, hygienic toilets?

What percentage of children enter primary school, and how many make it to secondary school? How many are put to work or married while still children? Do they enter adolescence equipped with the knowledge to protect themselves against HIV?

The data show that tremendous progress has been made during the past few decades:

- About 90 million children who would have died if mortality rates had stuck at their 1990 level have, instead, lived past the age of five.[1]

1   United Nations Children's Fund, *Committing to Child Survival: A Promise Renewed, Progress Report 2013*, UNICEF, New York, 2013, p. 12, <http://www.unicef.org/publications/files/APR_Progress_Report_2013_9_Sept_2013.pdf>, accessed 18 December 2013.

- Deaths from measles among children under five years of age fell from 482,000 in 2000 to 86,000 in 2012, thanks in large part to immunisation coverage, which increased from 16 per cent in 1980 to 84 per cent in 2012.[2]

- Improvements in nutrition have led to a 37 per cent drop in stunting since 1990.[3]

- Primary school enrolment has increased, even in the least-developed countries: whereas in 1990 only 53 per cent of children in those countries gained school admission, by 2011 the rate had improved to 81 per cent.[4]

- Nearly 1.9 billion people have gained access to improved sanitation since 1990.[5]

But the tables also bear witness to ongoing violations of children's rights:

2   UNICEF analysis based on UN Inter-agency Group for Child Mortality Estimation (IGME), 2013, drawing on provisional analyses by the World Health Organization and Child Epidemiology Reference Group (CHERG), 2013.

3   United Nations Children's Fund, *Committing to Child Survival: A Promise Renewed, Progress Report 2013*, UNICEF, New York, 2013, p. 27.

4   Report of the Secretary-General on the work of the Organization, A/68/1, United Nations, New York, 2013, p. 34.

5   World Health Organization and United Nations Children's Fund *Joint Monitoring Programme (JMP) for Water Supply and Sanitation, Progress on Sanitation and Drinking-Water: 2013 Update*, World Health Organization and UNICEF, Geneva, 2013, p.4, <http://www.wssinfo.org/fileadmin/user_upload/resources/JMPreport2013.pdf>, accessed 18 December 2013.

- Some 6.6 million children under five years of age died in 2012, mostly from preventable causes, their fundamental right to survive and develop unrealised.

- 15 per cent of the world's children[6] engage in child labour that compromises their right to protection from economic exploitation and infringes on their right to learn and play.

- 11 per cent of girls are married before they turn 15,[7] jeopardizing their rights to health, education and protection.

- The right to freedom from cruel and degrading punishment is violated whenever children are subjected to violent discipline at home or in school.

The tables also reveal gaps and inequities, showing that gains and deprivations are unevenly distributed. Children's chances differ depending on whether their country is a rich or a poor one; whether they are born girls or boys, into families rich or poor; or whether they live in the countryside or the city – and there, too, whether they live in well-to-do areas or impoverished neighbourhoods.

Of the roughly 18,000 children under five years old who die every day, a disproportionate number are from

6   Figure excludes China.

7   Figure excludes China.

parts of cities or the countryside that are cut off from services because of poverty or geography. Many could be saved by proven means and at little cost.

Although diarrhoea can be treated effectively and inexpensively with oral rehydration salts, children from the richest homes who become ill with diarrhoea are up to four times more likely to be treated than children from the poorest homes.[8] And while improved drinking water has become available to 2.1 billion more people worldwide since 1990,[9] this progress has bypassed many residents of rural areas. They account for less than half of the world's population but make up 83 per cent of those still deprived of a reliable source of safe drinking water.

Data that reveal disparities masked by aggregate figures can help to direct interventions that can reach the unreached and right the wrong of exclusion. The more precisely aid and opportunity can be focused, the greater the potential impact.

Data for children's rights

The world will commemorate the 25th anniversary of the Convention on the Rights of the Child (CRC) in November 2014, and the culmination of the Millennium Development Goals (MDGs) in 2015. Both will be occasions to celebrate the progress made for children and to recommit to reaching the millions of children whose rights are not yet fulfilled.

Data have played a key role in achieving that progress and are essential in identifying the most disadvantaged of the world's 2.2 billion children, understanding the barriers they confront, and designing and monitoring initiatives that make it possible for every child to realise her or his rights.

Telling untold stories

Being counted makes children visible, and this act of recognition makes it possible to address their needs and advance their rights.

In the Democratic Republic of the Congo, for example, the 2010 MICS found that only 28 per cent of births had been registered. Rapid surveys modelled on UNICEF's Monitoring Results for Equity Systems framework further revealed that the denial of the right to an official identity led to more deprivations – denying access to health, education and other services.

Action plans developed and implemented with community involvement led to a surge in birth registration – in one district, from six per cent in June 2012 to 41 per cent in December 2012.

Pregnant women also benefited: 58 per cent received at least four antenatal care visits, up from 16 per cent six months earlier.[10]

But not all children are being counted, and not to be counted only perpetuates invisibility and voicelessness. This puts children at greater risk. Groups commonly undercounted or overlooked include children living in institutions or temporary housing, children in detention, children living and working on the street, children with disabilities, trafficked children, migrant children, internally displaced and refugee children, and children from ethnic minorities living in remote areas or following a nomadic or pastoralist way of life.[11]

Many children in these categories experience intersecting forms of discrimination and deprivation. Data collected must be further broken down to reveal how marginalisation on account of disability, detention or migration, for example, is also affected by such factors as wealth, sex or where a child lives.

January 2014

⇨ The above information is reprinted with kind permission from UNICEF. Please visit www.unicef.org for further information.

© UNICEF 2014

8   Committee on the Rights of the Child, General guidelines regarding the form and contents of periodic reports to be submitted by States Parties under article 44, paragraph 1(b), of the Convention, 11 October 1996, <http://www.childoneurope.org/issues/crc_committee/su06-General-Guidelines-for-Periodic-Reports.pdf>, accessed 18 December 2013.

9   Committee on the Rights of the Child, Convention on the Rights of the Child General Comment No.5 (2003): General measures of implementation of the Convention on the Rights of the Child (arts. 4, 42 and 44, para. 6), p. 12 (48), 27 November 1993, <http://daccess-dds-ny.un.org/doc/UNDOC/GEN/G03/455/14/PDF/G0345514.pdf?OpenElement>, accessed 18 December 2013.

10 United Nations Children's Fund, Democratic Republic of the Congo submission.

11 Martorano, Bruno, Luisa Natali, Chris de Neubourg and Jonathan Bradshaw (2013), 'Child wellbeing in advanced economies in the late 2000s,' Working Paper 2013-01, UNICEF Office of Research, Florence, p. 40, <http://www.unicef-irc.org/publications/pdf/iwp_2013_1.pdf>, accessed 18 December 2013.

All rights, every child

In creating the Convention on the Rights of the Child (CRC), the international community has recognised that children are people who have rights that must be respected equally to those of adults.

Four main principles form the core of the CRC:

⇨ Non-discrimination or universality (article 2): All children have rights, regardless of race, colour, sex, language, religion, political or other opinion, national, ethnic or social origin, property, disability, birth or other status.

⇨ Best interests (article 3): The child's best interests must be a primary consideration in all decisions affecting her or him.

⇨ Life, survival and development (article 6): All children have a right to life, and to survive and develop – physically, mentally, spiritually, morally, psychologically and socially – to their full potential.

⇨ Respect for the views of the child (article 12): Children have the right to express themselves freely on matters that affect them, and to have their views taken seriously.

By articulating children's rights and obliging States Parties to respect, protect and fulfil them, the CRC provides a strong impetus for the collection, analysis and dissemination of data.

In order to survive and develop to their full potential, children need health care, nutritious food, education that nurtures their minds and equips them with useful knowledge and skills, freedom from violence and exploitation, and the time and space to play. The right to life, survival and development thus points to a wide range of indicators that must be measured in order to make sure that this right is realised.

Combating discrimination and inequity entails identifying children who are discriminated against and excluded from services and opportunities. To this end, the Committee on the Rights of the Child, the body charged with tracking implementation of the CRC, has urged that data be disaggregated by age, sex, urban and rural residence, membership in minority or indigenous groups, ethnicity, religion, disability and 'any other category considered appropriate'.

The Committee has further emphasised that it is not enough to collect data. In order to identify problems and inform policies, the data also need to be analysed, disseminated to the public and used to assess progress in realising children's rights.

The CRC's guarantee of the right to be heard requires that adults who make decisions affecting children's lives listen to children deeply and seriously, giving due respect and consideration to their views. Children therefore need safe, meaningful opportunities to participate in research, as well as access to the fruits of data collection and analysis.

January 2014

⇨ The above information is reprinted with kind permission from UNICEF. Please visit www.unicef.org for further information.

Out-of-school children and child labour

An extract from the 2014 Policy Paper by Global March.

1. Education for all – all girls and boys in school

The right to education – like all human rights – is universal and inalienable. Fully realising the right to education is a holistic one, encompassing access to education, inclusive education, educational quality and the environment in which education is provided. Further, education as a human right places the prime responsibility for its realisation on the states who are the custodians of all human rights with the duty to respect, protect and fulfil human rights. In terms of primary education, states are obliged to ensure free and compulsory education for all.

Education is one of the most powerful tools for transforming human lives, nations, society and world at large. Equipped and empowered with knowledge and skills through education, children and youth can give wings to their dreams, becoming teachers, musicians, mathematicians, scientists, doctors, artists, farmers and many such capable and productive members of society upon adulthood.

Education provides a compelling case for development. A recently completed study from 50 countries established that every extra year of schooling provided to the whole population can increase average annual GDP growth by 0.37%. Another survey of 120 countries from between 1970–2000 provides compelling evidence that education consistently and significantly boosts economic development and is a necessary precondition for long-term economic growth. Further, by making people more skilled and employable, education can provide an escape route from poverty. In low-income countries, an additional year of education adds about 10% to a person's income on average. Education also plays an important role in promoting good health. Children of more educated mothers are less likely to be stunted or underweight due to malnutrition, and educated mothers are more likely to give birth in safe conditions. Education can reduce the spread of HIV by promoting safe sexual behaviour. Investing in girls' education and reaching the goal of gender parity would enable gender equality elsewhere in society, such as in the labour market. Lastly, education has effects far beyond the classroom. Through education, societies foster values, spread ideas and equip their citizens with skills for participation in society. Education also promotes tolerance and understanding between people – both individually and on a national level thus fostering peace (EFA GMR Policy Paper June 2012). Sadly, we are far from reaping these and many more benefits of education as many children are missing out on a chance to be in school, learn and receive education.

As the Education For All (EFA) process is progressing, two main groups of children are still left behind. First, children who have yet to gain access to a good primary school. Second, those who do not get to attend even when a basic primary school is accessible: these are referred to as the 'hard-to-reach children' among the out-of-school children. According to the most recent figures released by the UNESCO Institute of Statistics (UIS), there were 57 million out-of-school children of primary school age in 2011, a slight decrease from 2010.

The focus of this article is on these 'hard-to-reach children', and within them the children who work instead of going to school for a complex set of reasons – child labourers.

To some children, the main obstacles to education are not school availability, cost or quality, but rather poverty, economic insecurity, discrimination and cultural practices. Furthermore, many children work, because child labour is perceived as the best use of their time and to prepare them for the life they are expected to lead.

Child labour and schooling is in many ways a nexus that is not easy to sort out. There is evidence to show that child labour depresses school enrolment rates, negatively affects school achievement, decreases graduation rates and inflates drop-out rates. Household poverty forces millions of children out of school and into paying jobs or – especially for young girls – domestic chores.

1.1 Out-of-school children

A total of 126 million primary and lower secondary aged children are out-of-school (UIS Fact Sheet, June 2013), translating to approximately 9% of all primary aged children out-of-school and 18% of lower secondary aged children missing out on an education. Girls are more excluded globally than boys, accounting for more than 50% of all out-of-school children in primary age group.

While the numbers of primary aged out-of-school children have declined from over 105 million in 1990, the progress has slowed and has eventually stagnated between 2008 and 2010. Of the 57 million primary aged children who were out-of-school in 2011 (UIS Fact Sheet, June 2013), 49% are expected to never enter school, and a further 23% have attended but left school. Furthermore, half of the out-of-school children (30 million) were in sub-Saharan Africa.

Children who are expected to never enter a school – 28 million of the global number of out-of-school children, i.e. 17 million girls and 11 million boys – are a serious challenge.

Alarmingly, the number of out-of-school children of primary school age increased in sub-Saharan Africa to 30 million in 2011 from 29 million in 2008, with Nigeria housing a third of all these children – an estimated 10.5 million out-of-school children.

Of the out-of-school children, regional data show large variations in patterns. In the Arab States, Central Asia, sub-Saharan Africa, and South and West Asia, about one-half of all out-of-school children will probably never enter school. In Latin America and the Caribbean, North America and

Western Europe, and Central and Eastern Europe, most out-of-school children will start school late. East Asia and the Pacific, as well as South and West Asia, have a large share of dropouts among their out-of-school populations.

Furthermore, it is estimated that there are 69 million out-of-school adolescents missing out on an education. South and West Asia have the largest numbers of out-of-school adolescents – 31.2 million. With 21.8 million out of school adolescents in sub-Saharan Africa, it has the highest percent (almost 36%) of adolescents out of school. Significant numbers are also present in East Asia and the Pacific, and Arab States. Adolescent girls are highly disadvantaged than their male counterparts, with an alarming 40% of adolescent girls out-of-school in sub-Saharan Africa and 30% in South and West Asia.

Typically, it is the marginalised, poor and remote rural populations, and those affected by conflict and discrimination, who are denied access to schooling. In short, the children who are being denied education are those who need it the most.

1.2 Hard-to-reach children

Children who do not go to school are children living in conditions of poverty, socio-cultural marginalisation, geographic isolation, racial and/or gender bias. Amongst others, hard-to-reach children include girls, children living with conflict/fragile states (who account for half the world's out-of-school children), children with disabilities, the rural poor, orphans and vulnerable children and working children (one in nine of the world's children are involved in child labour – accounting for 168 million children). Their exclusion from education is simply one more manifestation of a web of rights violations. Without access to good quality education, children are denied the opportunity to acquire knowledge, capabilities and self-confidence necessary to act on their own behalf in changing the circumstances which are excluding them.

Hard-to-reach children face one or a combination of obstacles to education, beyond whether or not good schools are available. It is these hard to reach children, including child labourers, which remains the great challenge. Economic factors are often thought to be important. Many poor families may indeed face problems covering even the smallest, informal fees, or simply cannot make it without the labour input or meagre

Year	Out-of-school children of primary school age	Progress in reduction of out-of-school children in primary school age (% change from previous year)
2000	102 million	–
2001	99 million	2.9%
2002	95 million	4%
2003	85 million	10.5%
2004	74 million	11%
2005	71 million	4%
2006	68 million	4.2%
2007	63 million	7.4%
2008	30 million	4.8%
2009	31 million	NA (numbers registered an increase by 1.7% in 2009)
2010	59 million	3.3%
2011	57 million	3.4%

earnings of the child. But the notion that observed household poverty is the main obstacle to schooling may have been exaggerated. The effect of fearing to fall into poverty is far less explored, and may be even more important to whether a child is sent to school or has to play a different role in the household risk mitigation strategy. Cultural norms and expectations may in many places turn out to explain more of the labour/schooling choice than anything else. When poverty and cultural norms interact, they may become effective obstacles to the inclusion and education of many vulnerable children.

With more children completing primary education, the demand for secondary education is growing. This increased demand poses a serious challenge for countries with limited resources. In sub-Saharan Africa, about one quarter of the children who complete primary school do not continue on to secondary education.

In some cultures, gender roles play a decisive part in explaining the labour and non-enrolment of girls. In combination with poverty, girls are given lower priority when a family must decide which children are

to be sent to school. Girls are also more vulnerable to be taken out of school to work during hardships.

School attendance figures provide evidence of the trade-off between child labour and Universal Primary Education (UPE). The Understanding Children's Work (UCW) Initiative has used household survey data to examine school attendance in some 60 countries.

Its findings indicate that working children face an attendance disadvantage of at least 10% in 28 countries, at least 20% in 15 countries and at least 30% in nine countries. Child labour is also associated with delayed school entry. In Cambodia for example a working child is 17% less likely to enter school at the official age and thus runs a higher risk of dropout.

2014

⇨ The above information is reprinted with kind permission from Global March Against Child Labour. Please visit www.globalmarch. org for further information.

© Global March Against Child Labour 2014

Who are child soldiers?

The internationally agreed definition for a child associated with an armed force or armed group (child soldier) is any person below 18 years of age who is, or who has been, recruited or used by an armed force or armed group in any capacity, including but not limited to children, boys and girls, used as fighters, cooks, porters, messengers, spies or for sexual purposes. It does not only refer to a child who is taking or has taken a direct part in hostilities.

(Paris Principles and Guidelines on Children Associated with Armed Forces or Armed Groups, 2007.)

A child soldier is anyone under the age of 18 who has been recruited or used in hostilities by state armed forces or non-state armed groups.

Since 2000, the participation of child soldiers has been reported in most armed conflicts and in almost every region of the world. Although there are no exact figures, and numbers continually change, tens of thousands of children under the age of 18 continue to serve in government forces or armed opposition groups. Some of those involved in armed conflict are under ten years old.

Both girls and boys are used in armed conflict and play a wide variety of roles. These can involve frontline duties including as fighters but they may also be used in other roles such as porters, couriers, spies, guards, suicide bombers or human shields, or to perform domestic duties such as cooking and cleaning. Girls and boys may also be used for sexual purposes by armed forces or groups.

Many children that participate in armed conflict are unlawfully recruited, either by force or at an age below that which is permitted in national law or international standards. Although international standards do not prohibit the voluntary recruitment of 16- and 17-year-olds by armed forces, it is contrary to best practice. Today close to two thirds of states recognise that banning under-18s from military ranks is necessary to protect them from the risk of involvement in armed conflict and to ensure their well-being, and that their other rights as children are respected.

Voices of children – Indonesia

'I know the work [monitoring the apparatus] is dangerous, and my parents had tried to stop me from getting involved. But I want to do something for the nanggroe therefore I was called for the fight. I am ready for all risks.'

Boy interviewed in March 2004: worked as an informant for the armed political group Free Aceh Movement, to spy on the Indonesian military when he was 17 years old.

International standards

Child Soldiers International promotes the adoption and implementation of international legal standards protecting children from military recruitment or use in hostilities. The following is a summary of the main international and regional legal standards relating to child soldiers:

1. International human rights law

Optional Protocol to the Convention on the Rights of the Child on the involvement of children in armed conflict (OPAC)

Adopted by the UN General Assembly on 25 May 2000, entered into force on 12 February 2002. OPAC sets 18 as the minimum age for direct participation in hostilities and for compulsory recruitment by state armed forces. States may accept volunteers from the age of 16 but must deposit a binding declaration at the time of ratification or accession, setting out their minimum voluntary recruitment age and outlining certain safeguards for such recruitment. OPAC also prohibits the recruitment or use in hostilities of under-18s by non-state armed groups.

Convention on the Rights of the Child

Adopted by the UN General Assembly on 20 November 1989, entered into force on 2 September 1990. The Convention on the Rights of the Child generally defines a child as any person under the age of 18. However, Article 38 uses the lower age of 15 as the minimum for recruitment or participation in armed conflict. This language is drawn from the

- PLENTY MORE WHERE THESE COME FROM ...

two Additional Protocols to the four Geneva Conventions of 1949 (see below).

Article 38 requires state parties to prevent anyone under the age of 15 from taking direct part in hostilities and to refrain from recruiting anyone under the age of 15 years. OPAC was drafted in order to raise the minimum ages set out in the Convention.

Implementation by State Parties of the Convention on the Rights of the Child and of its optional protocols to the Convention, including OPAC, is monitored by the (UN) Committee on the Rights of the Child.

2. International criminal law

Rome Statute of the International Criminal Court: The Rome Statute establishes a permanent criminal court to try persons charged with committing war crimes, crimes against humanity and genocide.

In its definition of war crimes the statute includes 'conscripting or enlisting children under the age of 15 years into national armed forces or using them to participate actively in hostilities' (Article 8(2)(b)(xxvi)) in international armed conflict; and in the case of an internal armed conflict, 'conscripting or enlisting children under the age of 15 years into armed forces or groups or using them to participate actively in hostilities' (Article 8(2)(e)(vii)).

The statute also defines sexual slavery as a war crime (Article 8(2) (b)(xxii) and Article 8(2)(e)(vii)) and a crime against humanity (Article 7(1) (g)). The treaty came into force and the court came into being on 1 July 2002.

3. International labour law

International Labour Organization (ILO) Minimum Age Convention 138: This convention was adopted on 26 June 1973 and came into force on 19 June 1976. States ratifying the convention are bound to: pursue a national policy designed to ensure the effective abolition of child labour; and raise progressively the minimum age for admission to employment or work to a level consistent with the fullest physical and mental development of young persons (Article 1). It also sets 18 years as 'the minimum age for admission to employment or work

which by its nature or circumstances in which it is carried out is likely to jeopardise the health, safety or morals of young persons' (Article 3).

International Labour Organization (ILO) Worst Forms of Child Labour Convention 182: This convention was adopted on 16 June 1999 and came into force on 19 November 2000. It commits each state which ratifies it to 'take immediate and effective measures to secure the prohibition and elimination of the worst forms of child labour as a matter of urgency'. The term 'child' applies to all persons under the age of 18 years, and the worst forms of child labour include forced or compulsory recruitment of children for use in armed conflict (Article 3a).

4. International humanitarian law

Additional Protocols to the four Geneva Conventions of 1949 (1977): The protocols set 15 as the minimum age for recruitment or use in armed conflict. This minimum standard applies to all parties, both governmental and non-governmental, in both international and internal armed conflict.

Article 77(2) of Additional Protocol I: applicable to international armed conflicts, states:

'The Parties to the conflict shall take all feasible measures in order that children who have not attained the age of 15 years do not take a direct part in hostilities and, in particular, they shall refrain from recruiting them into their armed forces. In recruiting among those persons who have attained the age of 15 years but who have not attained the age of 18 years the Parties to the conflict shall endeavour to give priority to those who are oldest.'

Article 4(3)(c) of the Additional Protocol II: applicable to non-international armed conflicts, states: 'Children who have not attained the age of 15 years shall neither be recruited in the armed forces or groups nor allowed to take part in hostilities.'

Customary international humanitarian law

Customary international law is made up of rules that come from 'a general

practice accepted as law' and that exist independent of treaty law.

Rules of customary international humanitarian law provide that 'children must not be recruited into armed forces or armed groups' and that 'children must not be allowed to take part in hostilities'. These rules apply to both international and non-international armed conflicts.

Additional Protocols I and II and the Rules of Customary International Humanitarian Law can be found on the ICRC website.

5. Regional standards

African Charter on the Rights and Welfare of the Child: The Charter is the only regional treaty which addresses the issue of child soldiers. It was adopted by the Organization of African Unity (now the African Union) and came into force in November 1999.

It defines a child as anyone below 18 years of age without exception. It also states that: 'States Parties to the present Charter shall take all necessary measures to ensure that no child shall take a direct part in hostilities and refrain in particular, from recruiting any child' (Article 22.2).

6. Principles relating to child soldiers

The Paris Commitments and Principles (2007): The Paris principles and guidelines on children associated with armed forces or armed groups (Paris Principles) and Paris commitments to protect children from unlawful recruitment or use by armed forces or armed groups (Paris Commitments) were formally endorsed by 58 states in 2007 at a meeting in France in February 2007. Their drafting followed a review of the 'Cape Town Principles and Best Practice on the prevention of recruitment of children into the armed forces and on demobilization and social reintegration of child soldiers in Africa', which had been the guiding principles on child soldiers since their adoption in 1997.

The aim of the Paris Principles and Commitments is to combat the unlawful recruitment or use of children by armed forces or armed groups. Their specific objective is to prevent the occurrence of this phenomenon, to secure the release of children concerned, to support their social reintegration and to ensure that they are afforded the greatest protection possible. In adhering to the Paris Commitments, states agree to uphold certain basic principles which will allow them to achieve the set objectives. The Paris Principles give more detailed guidelines on the implementation of the Commitments. As at September 2011, 100 states had endorsed the Paris Commitments.

7. UN Security Council children and armed conflict framework

The UN Security Council has passed a series of resolutions condemning the recruitment and use of children in hostilities. These are resolutions 1261 (1999), 1314 (2000), 1379 (2001), 1460 (2003), 1539 (2004) and 1612 (2005), 1882 (2009) and 1998 (2011) on children and armed conflict. Resolutions can be found on the UN Security Council website.

Security Council Resolution 1379 (2001) called upon the UN Secretary-General to list parties that recruit and use children in the annual report on children and armed conflict. Killing and maiming and sexual violence in conflict (Resolution 1882 in 2009) and attacks on schools and hospitals (Resolution 1998 in 2011), were later added as criteria for listing.

Security Council Resolution 1460 (2003) requires listed parties to enter into talks with the United Nations to agree clear and time bound action plans to end child recruitment and use. The concept of action plans is now also applied more broadly to other grave violations against children for which parties can be listed.

To date, 17 listed parties have signed action plans, including five government forces and 12 non-state armed groups. Of these, five have fully complied with the action plan and were subsequently de-listed.

Security Council Resolution 1612 established the monitoring and reporting mechanism (MRM) on grave violations against children in armed conflict. The purpose of the MRM is to provide for the systematic gathering of accurate, timely and objective information on grave violations committed against children in armed conflict.

Security Council Resolution 1612 (2005) also established the Security Council Working Group on Children and Armed Conflict which consists of the 15 Security Council members. The Working Group reviews UN Secretary-General reports on children in armed conflict in specific country situations and makes recommendations to parties to conflict, Governments and donors, as well as UN actors on measures

to promote the protection of war-affected children.

For information on action plans, MRM and the Security Council Working Group see the website of the Special Representative of the Secretary-General for Children and Armed Conflict.

8. Special Representative of the Secretary-General for Children and Armed Conflict

The Special Representative of the Secretary-General for Children and Armed Conflict serves as an independent advocate for the protection and well-being of children affected by armed conflict, working with partners to enhance their protection and facilitating through diplomatic and humanitarian initiatives the work of operational actors on the ground. The mandate of the SRSG was first established by UN General Assembly resolution 51/77 of 12 December 1996.

⇨ The above information is reprinted with kind permission from Child Soldiers International. Please visit www.child-soldiers.org for further information.

UK under fire for recruiting an 'army of children'

MOD finds itself in the company of countries such as North Korea over use of teenage soldiers.

The figures, released last week, have sparked renewed criticism of the British Army's use of boy soldiers. Following an outcry over the deployment of 17-year-olds to the Gulf War in 1991, and to Kosovo in 1999, the Army amended its rules stopping soldiers under 18 from being sent on operations where there was a possibility of fighting. Despite this, at least 20 soldiers aged 17 are known to have served in Afghanistan and Iraq due to errors by the MoD.

Critics claim the figures mean Britain stands alongside some of the world's most repressive regimes by recruiting children into the armed forces – among under 20 countries, including North Korea and Iran, that allow 16-year-olds to join up. They accused the MoD of deliberately targeting teenagers not old enough to vote in a bid to boost recruitment.

There are more than 1,700 teenagers in the armed forces below voting age. The vast majority of 16- and 17-year-olds are in the Army, according to the 2014 annual personnel report. And the proportion of Army recruits aged just 16 has risen from ten per cent in 2012–13 to 13 per cent in 2013–14. Many of them would have begun the enlistment process when they were 15, according to campaigners.

'By recruiting at 16, the UK isolates itself from its main political and military allies and finds itself instead sharing a policy with the likes of North Korea and Iran. These are not states which the UK would normally want its military to be associated with,' said Richard Clarke, director of Child Soldiers International.

And Paola Uccellari, director of Children's Rights Alliance for England, said: 'Targeting children for recruitment into the armed forces puts them at risk of serious and irreparable harm. The Government should not rely on children to plug gaps in the armed forces.'

Despite mounting pressure internationally, with UN bodies such as UNICEF, the Committee on the Rights of the Child, and the UN Secretary-General's Special Representative for Children and Armed Conflict all in favour of the recruitment age being raised to 18, the MoD continues to take on 16-year-olds.

'Research has shown that 16-year-old recruits are much more likely than adults to suffer bullying and harassment, to develop serious mental health problems, to be injured in training, and to be killed once they reach deployable age,' added Mr Clarke. 'The MoD might think that it's a quick fix to use children to fill the Army roles adults don't want to do, but it's unethical and operationally unsound,' he said.

Critics believe a mounting military recruitment crisis in the armed forces is one reason behind the increases. Plans to create tens of thousands of reservists to fill the gap left by mass redundancies of serving soldiers are understood to be well behind expectations. Reserves currently number 22,010, an increase of 30 compared with 12 months ago. At the current rate of recruitment, it will take more than four centuries to meet the target of a 35,000-strong reserve force by 2018.

'At least 20 soldiers aged 17 are known to have served in Afghanistan and Iraq due to errors by the MoD'

An MoD spokesperson dismissed the concerns as 'nonsense'. 'A career in the armed forces provides young people with benefits and opportunities, equipping them with valuable and transferable skills for life, so it is encouraging that young people continue to recognise this and are coming forward to serve their country.' The MoD has 'procedures in place to ensure no one under 18 may join our armed forces without the formal written consent of their parent or guardian and no one under 18 can deploy on operations'.

Colonel Richard Kemp, former commander of British forces in Afghanistan, defended the practice of recruiting 16-year-olds. 'Some of the finest soldiers I commanded during my 30 years in the Army started their careers as juniors, enlisting at 16.' The approach 'unquestionably boosts the quality and fighting effectiveness of the armed forces'. He added: 'Calling this scheme unethical and operationally unsound not only betrays Child Soldiers International's ignorance of military matters but also insults the young men and women who serve their country with courage, pride and distinction.'

But Madeleine Moon MP, a member of the Commons Defence Select Committee, described the increase in recruitment of under-18s as 'alarming'. 'The failure to recruit adults should not be used as an excuse to flood the Army with vulnerable youngsters.'

25 May 2014

⇨ The above information is reprinted with kind permission from *The Independent*. Please visit www.independent.co.uk for further information.

A girl's right to say no to marriage

Working to end child marriage and keep girls in school.

Child marriage is a violation of children's human rights. Despite being prohibited by international human rights law and many national laws, child marriage continues to rob millions of girls around the world of their childhood. It forces them out of education and into a life of poor prospects, with increased risk of violence, abuse, ill health or early death. While boys are also married as children, child marriage affects girls in greater numbers and with consequences which can be devastating for their health and well-being.

A global problem

One in three girls in the developing world will be married by their eighteenth birthday.[1] If nothing is done to stop current trends, more than 140 million girls will be married as children by 2020. That's 14 million every year or nearly 39,000 girls married every day.[2]

Underpinning child marriage is a combination of poverty, gender inequality and a lack of protection for children's rights. These drivers are frequently compounded by limited access to quality educational and employment opportunities and reinforced by entrenched social norms.

Poverty and geography: drivers of child marriage

Girls from the poorest 20 per cent of households are over three times more likely to marry before they are 18 than those from the richest homes.[3]

In developing countries, girls in rural areas are twice as likely to be married by 18 as those in urban areas.[4]

There is a growing international consensus on the severe impact which child marriage has on children's rights and that it often constitutes a barrier to realising girls' right to education. It is also clear that education is key to delaying marriage, to giving girls more choices and opportunities,' and enabling them to develop their full potential.

Plan[5] is calling for urgent, concerted and integrated action at local, national and international levels to enable millions of girls to avoid child marriage, stay in school and benefit from a quality education.

The toll on health and well-being

Child marriage is a public health issue as well as a human rights violation. Girls married early are more likely to experience violence, abuse and forced sexual relations. They are more vulnerable to sexually transmitted infections (including HIV) and have reduced levels of sexual and reproductive health.[6]

1 UNFPA, Marrying Too Young: End Child Marriage, New York: UNFPA, 2012

2 Ibid.

3 According to UNFPA data, more than half (54 per cent) of girls in the poorest 20 per cent of households are child brides, compared with only 16 per cent of girls in the richest 20 per cent of households. UNFPA, Marrying Too Young: End Child Marriage, New York: UNFPA, 2012

4 UNFPA, Marrying Too Young: End Child Marriage, New York: UNFPA, 2012

5 An international child rights organisation

6 IPPF, UNFPA, The Global Coalition on Women and AIDS, Ending Child Marriage: A Guide For Global Policy Action, IPPF: London, 2006

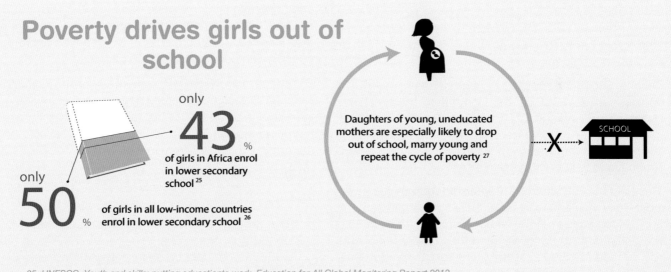

Poverty drives girls out of school

only **43**% of girls in Africa enrol in lower secondary school[25]

only **50**% of girls in all low-income countries enrol in lower secondary school[26]

Daughters of young, uneducated mothers are especially likely to drop out of school, marry young and repeat the cycle of poverty[27]

SCHOOL

25. UNESCO, Youth and skills: putting educationto work, Education for All Global Monitoring Report 2012, Paris: UNESCO, 2012
26. Ibid.
27. UNICEF, Early Marriage: A Harmful Traditional Practice, New York: UNICEF, 2005

Early pregnancy is one of the most dangerous causes and consequences of child marriage. Girls who become pregnant at a young age face higher risks of maternal mortality and morbidity.[7]

> **'More than 140 million girls will become child brides by 2020, if current rates of child marriage continue'**

Pregnancy during the first years after puberty increases the risk of miscarriage, obstructed labour, post-partum haemorrhage, pregnancy-related hypertension and lifelong debilitating conditions such as obstetric fistula.[8]

Maternal and infant mortality

Every year, nearly 13.7 million 15- to 19-year-old girls in the developing world give birth while married.[9] Complications in pregnancy and childbirth are the leading cause of mortality for girls aged 15 to 19 in developing countries.[10]

Infant deaths are 50 per cent higher among babies born to mothers under 20 than among those born to women in their twenties.[11]

Babies born to adolescent mothers are more likely to be stillborn, premature, underweight and at increased risk of dying in infancy due to the mother's young age. This risk is compounded by a lack of access to comprehensive sexual and reproductive health information and services.[12]

Child marriage also means that children are often vulnerable and socially isolated from their own family and friends, with little or no support for dealing with marriage, parenthood, domestic and family duties.

Prevention through education

Education is widely considered to be one of the most important factors in delaying the age of marriage for girls.[13] In developing countries, evidence shows that the more education a girl receives, the less likely she is to be married before the age of 18 and the more likely she is to delay pregnancy and childbirth.[14]

Education is key to ending child marriage

Girls with no education are three times as likely to marry by 18 as those with a secondary or higher education.[15] Nearly 70 per cent of girls with no education were married by the age of 18 in the 25 countries with the highest prevalence of child marriage.[16]

All girls have a right to a quality education – one which does not reinforce gender stereotypes, but which is relevant to their needs and aspirations and promotes

7 UNICEF, State of the World's Children, Realizing the Rights of Adolescents, New York: UNICEF, 2011

8 Gordon Brown, Out of wedlock, into school: combating child marriage through education, London: The Office of Gordon and Sarah Brown, 2012

9 Based on UNFPA data that 'every year, nearly 16 million adolescent girls aged 15–19 years old give birth; about 95 per cent of these births occur in low- and middle-income countries. Ninety per cent of these adolescent mothers in developing countries are married.'

10 UNFPA, Marrying Too Young: End Child Marriage, New York: UNFPA, 2012

11 WHO, WHO Guidelines on Preventing Early Pregnancy and Poor Reproductive Health Outcomes Among Adolescents In Developing Countries, Geneva: WHO, 2011

12 Ibid.

13 International Centre for Research on Women, New Insights on Preventing Child Marriage: A Global Analysis of Factors and Programs, Washington DC: ICRW, 2007

14 UNFPA, Marrying Too Young: End Child Marriage, New York: UNFPA, 2012

15 Ibid.

16 UNFPA, Marrying Too Young: End Child Marriage, New York: UNFPA, 2012

National laws discriminate against girls

Child marriage costs lives

50,000

The number of teenagers who die of pregnancy and birth complications every year [28]

146 countries   105 countries

The number of countries where marriage before 18 is legal with parental consent, per sex [29]

28. UNICEF, Progress for Children: A Report Card for Adolescents, New York: UNICEF, 2012
29. UNFPA, Marrying Too Young: End Child Marriage, New York: UNFPA, 2012

gender equality and human rights. Learning in a safe and supportive environment enables girls to develop the skills, knowledge and confidence to claim their rights. It gives them the chance to reach their full potential and to assert their autonomy, helping them to make free and informed decisions about their life, including whether, when and who to marry, along with decisions affecting their sexual and reproductive health.

'Girls with no education are three times more likely to marry before 18 than those with a secondary or higher education'

Yet, in low-income countries, only 50 per cent of girls are enrolled in lower secondary school, with 39 per cent enrolled in secondary school.[17] Social, domestic and economic pressures too often force adolescent girls out of secondary school. The costs

associated with schooling increase – and girls are thought ready for marriage, child-bearing and domestic duties. They drop out at the very time when education could guide them through the vulnerable period of adolescence.[18]

Marriage pregnancy and school drop-out

Marriage and pregnancy have been identified as some of the key factors forcing girls to leave school. Girls often lack basic literacy and numeracy skills because they have to drop out. Each year of marriage before adulthood reduces a girl's literacy by 5.6 percentage points.[19]

Financial barriers and harmful gender norms can drive parents to prioritise sons' education over that of daughters' – often on the assumption that girls will marry soon anyway. Many parents also fear for their daughters' safety in school. The onset of puberty makes girls more vulnerable to sexual violence, harassment and abuse by teachers, staff and other pupils.[20]

Poor teaching and unsupportive environments make girls less likely to pass critical examinations needed to access higher levels of education.[21]

⇨ The above information is reprinted with kind permission from Plan. Please visit www.plan-international.org for further information.

© Plan 2014

'Child marriage is a serious human rights violation, not just a development issue'

17 UNESCO, Youth and skills: putting education to work, Education for All Global Monitoring Report 2012, Paris: UNESCO, 2012

18 Plan International, Because I am a Girl, Africa Report. Progress and Obstacles to Girls' Education in Africa, Woking: Plan International, 2012

19 UNGEI, Child Marriage and Education: A Major Challenge, New York: UNGEI, 2012

20 Plan International, Learn Without Fear. The Global Campaign to End Violence in Schools, Woking: Plan International, 2008

21 Plan UK, DFID PPA-funded 'Building skill for life for adolescent girls' programme: global baseline report, prepared for Plan UK by the Royal Tropical Institute, London: Plan UK, 2012

39,000 girls under 18 are married every day

18 and under
34%
That's 1 in 3 girls

15 and under
12%
That's 1 in 9 girls

⟨th⟩e percentage of girls married in developing countries[22]

more than
60%
of women are married by 18 in the four countries where child marriage is most common[23]

. Excluding China. UNFPA, Marrying Too Young: End Child Marriage, New York: UNFPA, 2012
. Among women aged 20–24. UNFPA, Marrying Too Young: End Child Marriage, New York: UNFPA, 2012

Child trafficking, exploitation on the rise, warns UN expert

In an increasingly interconnected world, children are more at risk than ever of being sexually exploited or sold, a United Nations independent expert warned today, calling for decisive steps at the global level to stop crimes such as child prostitution and trafficking.

'Millions of girls and boys worldwide are victims of sexual exploitation, even though this issue in recent years has gained increased visibility,' said Najat Maalla M'jid, the Special Rapporteur on the sale of children, child prostitution and child pornography, as she presented her final report to the 25th session of the Human Rights Council, which opened last week and is to wrap on 28 March.

Social tolerance and impunity, persistent demand and the lucrative aspect of this trade for global criminal networks are only some of the factors that make children increasingly vulnerable, she said, adding that 'the ongoing development of new technologies has made access to children in all parts of the world easier and increased exploitation'.

The availability of child pornography online is growing. 'Child victims of online sexual exploitation are younger and younger, and the images are more and more horrific,' explained Ms Maalla M'jid, whose report provides an overview of the main issues and trends relating to her six-year-long mandate.

The Special Rapporteur stressed that certain forms of sexual exploitation are increasing such as trafficking of children for sexual and economic purposes, child sex tourism and online child sexual exploitation, but noted that the true scope of the problem was not clear due to inadequate legislation, lack of reliable data, and under-reporting.

'The clandestine nature of such exploitation, the fear of reprisals and stigmatisation, as well as the lack of child-sensitive complaints mechanisms, also hampers our understanding of these crimes,' she said.

'The destinations for child sex tourism are continually changing, as perpetrators tend to choose countries with weak legislation and controls,' noted the UN expert.

In her presentation, Ms Maalla M'jid drew attention to the 'serious and long-lasting physical, psychological and social effects, not only for the girls and boys who are the direct victims, but also for their families and communities,' regretting that this impact is not sufficiently understood and taken into account when addressing recovery, remedies and compensation.

'Despite significant efforts and reiterated global commitments, much still needs to be done to protect, rehabilitate and reintegrate victims, provide reparation to children for the damage they have suffered, sanction those responsible, change certain social norms, and to ultimately prevent such exploitation,' the expert said, urging the international community to establish a global response, through a global legal framework and sustainable transnational co-operation. In addition, Ms Maalla M'jid called for close co-operation with the private sector, and for strong corporate social responsibility among Internet service providers, telecommunications, tourism and travel industry, media and financial institutions.

'Children must also be involved in assessing the scale of the problem and developing solutions,' she added.

'As the world reflects on universal development goals for the post-2015 era, bearing in mind the strong connections between economic, social, and political development and child protection issues, child-sensitive protection must be included in the post-2015 development agenda,' the Special Rapporteur concluded.

Independent experts or special rapporteurs are appointed by the Geneva-based UN Human Rights Council to examine and report back on a country situation or a specific human rights theme. The positions are honorary and the experts are not UN staff, nor are they paid for their work.

13 March 2014

⇨ The above information is reprinted with kind permission from the UN News Centre. Please visit www.un.org/news for further information.

© UN News Centre 2014

Child sexual exploitation

What is child sexual exploitation? How are children and young people affected? What can we do about it?

There is still a great deal we don't know about the extent of child sexual exploitation (CSE), its long-term impact on victims and the effectiveness of treatment and prevention. However, we do know that it is child abuse and interventions must be appropriate and timely. These pages aim to provide an introduction to the subject and a guide to the policy, practice and research as well as useful resources for anyone working with children or with an interest in child protection.

What is child sexual exploitation?

Child sexual exploitation (CSE) is a form of sexual abuse that involves the manipulation and/or coercion of young people under the age of 18 into sexual activity in exchange for things such as money, gifts, accommodation, affection or status. The manipulation or 'grooming' process involves befriending children, gaining their trust, and often feeding them drugs and alcohol, sometimes over a long period of time, before the abuse begins. The abusive relationship between victim and perpetrator involves an imbalance of power which limits the victim's options. It is a form of abuse which is often misunderstood by victims and outsiders as consensual. Although it is true that the victim can be tricked into believing they are in a loving relationship, no child under the age of 18 can ever consent to being abused or exploited (Barnardo's, 2012).

Child sexual exploitation can manifest itself in different ways. It can involve an older perpetrator exercising financial, emotional or physical control over a young person. It can involve peers manipulating or forcing victims into sexual activity, sometimes within gangs and in gang-affected neighbourhoods, but not always. Exploitation can also involve opportunistic or organised networks of perpetrators who may profit financially from trafficking young victims between different locations to engage in sexual activity with multiple men (Barnardo's, 2011).

This abuse often involves violent and degrading sexual assaults and rape. The Children's Commissioner's report on sexual exploitation by gangs and groups found that oral and anal rape were the most frequently reported types of abuse. Experts agree that these types of abuse are particularly humiliating and controlling, and, as such, may be preferred by those who exploit vulnerable young people (Berelowitz et al., 2012). Exploitation can also occur without physical contact when children are persuaded or forced to post indecent images of themselves online, participate in non-contact sexual activities via a webcam or smartphone, or engage in sexual conversations on a mobile phone (DfE, 2011).

Technology is widely used by perpetrators as a method of grooming and coercing victims, often through social networking sites and mobile devices (Jago et al., 2011). This form of abuse usually occurs in private, or in semi-public places such as parks, cinemas, cafes and hotels. It is increasingly occurring at 'parties' organised by perpetrators for the purposes of giving victims drugs and alcohol before sexually abusing them (Barnardo's, 2012).

If you suspect or discover that someone is sexually exploiting a child you can discuss your concerns with one of our counsellors by calling 0808 800 5000 or e-mailing help@nspcc.org.uk.

How much child sexual exploitation is there?

It is not possible to say exactly how many young people are victims of child sexual exploitation for a number of reasons. It is described as a 'hidden' form of abuse which leaves victims confused, frightened and reluctant to make any disclosures. Some young people are not even aware they are experiencing abuse as the perpetrator has manipulated them into believing they are in a loving relationship, or that they are dependent on their abuser for protection (Sharp, N., 2011; Cockbain, E. and Brayley, H., 2012; Child Exploitation and Online Protection Centre (CEOP), 2011). There is also no recognised category of abuse for sexual exploitation in child protection procedures and data relating to CSE cases is often partial, incomplete, concealed in other categories of data, or simply unrecorded (Berelowitz et al., 2012; CEOP, 2012). In addition, when perpetrators are convicted for involvement in child sexual exploitation cases, it is for associated offences such as sexual activity with a child – there is no specific crime of child sexual exploitation and therefore it is not possible to obtain figures from police statistics of sexual offences (Berelowitz et al., 2012).

A UK-wide survey estimated that in 2009–2010, there were over 3,000 young people accessing services because they had been affected by sexual exploitation. In a thematic assessment, CEOP received over 2,000 reports of victims from local authorities and police forces. The Children's Commissioner's inquiry in to sexual exploitation by groups and gangs confirmed 2,049 reported victims in the 14 month period from August 2010 to October 2011. Furthermore, the Children's Commissioner's inquiry estimated from the evidence that 16,500 children in the UK were at risk of sexual exploitation. For the reasons outlined above, figures of reported victims are just the tip of the iceberg (Barnardo's, 2012; Berelowitz et al., 2012; CEOP, 2011).

What are the signs and symptoms of child sexual exploitation?

Grooming and sexual exploitation can be very difficult to identify. Warning signs can easily be mistaken for 'normal' teenage behaviour and/or development. However, parents, carers, school teachers and practitioners are advised to be alert to the following signs and symptoms:

⇨ inappropriate sexual or sexualised behaviour

⇨ repeat sexually transmitted infections; in girls repeat pregnancy, abortions, miscarriage

⇨ having unaffordable new things (clothes, mobile) or expensive habits (alcohol, drugs)

⇨ going to hotels or other unusual locations to meet friends

⇨ getting in/out of different cars driven by unknown adults

⇨ going missing from home or care

⇨ having older boyfriends or girlfriends

⇨ associating with other young people involved in sexual exploitation

⇨ truancy, exclusion, disengagement with school, opting out of education altogether

⇨ unexplained changes in behaviour or personality (chaotic, aggressive, sexual)

⇨ drug or alcohol misuse

⇨ getting involved in crime

⇨ injuries from physical assault, physical restraint, sexual assault

(Barnardo's, 2011; CEOP, 2011; Berelowitz et al., 2012).

This is not an exhaustive list and indicators can change over time. For a fuller list see our factsheet on identifying children and young people sexually exploited through street grooming.

There are also a number of risk factors which can make a child vulnerable to sexual exploitation, these will be discussed in 'What do we know about the victims?' on page 34.

What are the causes of child sexual exploitation?

It has been suggested that offenders who sexually exploit children and young people do it not only for the opportunity to commit sexual offences, but also for the satisfaction of manipulating and controlling someone vulnerable. In this respect, they have been compared to

perpetrators of domestic violence. Further research would be needed to establish this link and explore fully the psychological motivation of these offenders (CEOP, 2011).

A study of gang associated sexual exploitation also observed that the abuse was a method for young men to exert power and control over young women. Other causes of this specific form of sexual exploitation include:

⇨ using sex as a means of initiating young people into a gang

⇨ sexual activity exchanged for status or protection

⇨ girls and young women used to entrap rival gang members

⇨ sexual assault as a weapon in conflict.

This study also found that girls and young women in this culture who are perceived to engage in casual sex, forfeit the right to refuse sex and are frequently forced by gang members. Previous experiences of sexual violence also increase a victim's

vulnerability to further abuse (Beckett, H. et al., 2012).

What do we know about the perpetrators?

According to the Children's Commissioner's Inquiry, there is a great deal that we do not know about perpetrators of child sexual exploitation. This is partly because agencies rarely record data on perpetrators and when they do it is inconsistent or incomplete. Frequently, victims only know their abusers by aliases and nicknames, or they can only provide physical descriptions. Furthermore, the circumstances in which children are abused often make it very difficult for them to identify their abusers. They describe 'parties' during which they were heavily intoxicated and/or drugged and sexually assaulted or raped by multiple men. Often they are moved from location to location and abused in each place. For these reasons, many abusers remain unidentified and the actual number of perpetrators is likely to be far higher than those reported (Berelowitz et al., 2012).

Of identified perpetrators, the vast majority were men and boys. The Children's Commissioner's study found that 72% were male, 10% were female and in 18% of cases the gender was undisclosed. The evidence for this study also indicated that the age range for perpetrators was 12 to 75 years. Perpetrators classified as 'White' formed the largest group, and those loosely recorded as 'Asian' formed the second largest group. Perpetrators from various other ethnic groups were also recorded (Berelowitz et al., 2012). Research also found that perpetrators of CSE within gangs were mainly men and boys aged between 13 and 25 years who took part in many forms of criminal activity in addition to sexual exploitation, including robbery and knife crime (Beckett, H. et al., 2012).

According to Barnardo's, eight of their child sexual exploitation services have reported an increase in exploitation by peers. In these cases, peers either abuse victims themselves or are indirectly responsible for the abuse by introducing victims to perpetrators. Some young people are involved in both direct and indirect abuse (Barnardo's, 2012). The Children's Commissioner's Inquiry found that of the 2,409 victims reported to them, 155 were also identified as perpetrators of child sexual exploitation (Berelowitz et al., 2012). According to CEOP, perpetrators can use one victim to gain access to others, asking victims to bring their friends along to pre-arranged meetings or 'parties'. These friends then fall victim to the exploitation themselves. In some cases, if victims try to break free of the abuse they are suffering, the perpetrator will deploy their peers to draw them back in (CEOP, 2011).

Perpetrators are often described as highly manipulative individuals who either create or exacerbate their victims' vulnerabilities such as isolation from families or friends, disengagement from services, or challenging or criminal behaviour. They do this in order to maintain control over their victims and distance them from people who may be able to protect them (CEOP, 2011).

What do we know about the victims?

Sexual exploitation can happen to any young person. It happens throughout the UK, in both urban and rural locations. It can happen to children of a range of ages, both male and female, from any ethnic background. Victims have identified as heterosexual, gay, lesbian and bisexual and some of them have been disabled or had learning difficulties. Sexual exploitation can happen to children from loving and secure families, although young people with additional vulnerabilities, such as experience of early childhood abuse, particularly sexual abuse, are at increased risk. The characteristics all victims have in common are their vulnerability and powerlessness (Berelowitz et al., 2012; Barnardo's, 2012).

CEOP's thematic assessment analysed 2,083 victims of child sexual exploitation. The vast majority were female, although in 31% of cases, the gender of the victim was unknown. It is believed that difficulty in recognising sexual exploitation in boys and young men has led to the under-representation of male victims. Victims most commonly came to the attention of statutory and non-statutory agencies at age 14 or 15 years, although victims can be as young as nine or ten years old. 61% of the victims were white, 33% were of unknown ethnicity, 3% were Asian and 1% of victims were black. Children from minority ethnic backgrounds face additional barriers in reporting and accessing services which could result in their under-representation in statistics (CEOP, 2011).

Researchers recognise that children who go missing and/or are in care are at heightened risk of sexual exploitation. CEOP's assessment found that in the 1,014 cases where this information was recorded, 842 children were reported as missing on at least one occasion. However, it is unknown whether these missing incidents preceded, coincided with, or followed the period of sexual exploitation. Of the 896 victims whose living situation was recorded, 311 were already in care when they began to be exploited and a further 43 were moved into care following intervention (CEOP, 2011).

A University College London study of 552 child sexual exploitation victims in Derby, found that nearly four out of ten had a history of criminal behaviour. Male victims (55%) were significantly more likely to offend than female victims (35%). Although there is a correlation between criminal activity and sexual exploitation, the data in this study did not suggest that the abuse causes offending; in some cases young people's criminal behaviour began around the time of the exploitation and in other cases offending and CSE were both features of the victim's 'generally chaotic lifestyle' (Cockbain, E. and Brayley, H., 2012).

Other risk factors associated with child sexual exploitation include:

⇨ parental substance use, domestic violence and parental mental health issues

⇨ history of abuse and/or neglect

⇨ recent bereavement or loss

⇨ links to a gang through relatives, peers or intimate relationships, or living in a gang-affected neighbourhood

⇨ associating with young people who are sexually exploited

⇨ homelessness

⇨ lacking friends from the same age group

⇨ low self-esteem or self-confidence

⇨ being a young carer

⇨ leaving care

(Berelowitz et al., 2012).

July 2013

⇨ The above information is reprinted with kind permission from the NSPCC. Please visit www.nspcc.org.uk/childsexualexploitation for further information and full references.

We have to learn more about the victims of child exploitation

Pam Lowe, Senior Lecturer in Sociology at Aston University

Mistakes were made, warning signs ignored and a general ignorance of and, in some cases, indifference to, child sexual exploitation meant that the grooming of young girls for sex had become 'widespread' and 'organised' in places such as Oxford and Rochdale, a home affairs committee report has found.

Child sexual exploitation has emerged in public discourse as a new category of 'crime'. A series of high-profile cases in areas such as Rochdale and Oxford have gained the public's attention. The term child sexual exploitation fits well into public discourse and we bring to this discussion existing ideas about childhood innocence, monstrous paedophiles and incompetent professionals that can be used. This is similar to the hunt for paedophiles within Operation Yewtree.

In fact, this particular style of story can be traced to the Victorian media when William Thomas Stead exposed stories of young women being plied with drink and drugs, bought and sold for sex, with a knowing police force turning a blind eye. Then, as now, this particular coverage led to a framing of debates in which some important elements got lost from public debate.

After all, there is no agreed definition of child sexual exploitation and no specific criminal offence in that name. So although the term is now used frequently, are we actually discussing the same thing? Unpacking what is happening is perhaps the first step towards understanding.

This is child prostitution

In general terms, there are three potential elements, which can be interconnected. The first issue is transaction sex, in other words exchanging items such as clothes, alcohol, drugs or phone credit for sexual activity. This can include survival sex, where it involves a place to stay or food to eat.

When young people (and adults) engage in transaction sex, neither the victim not perpetrator may consider this exploitation at all. They believe they are getting a deal whether this is a lift into town from a taxi-driver, or the latest phone from an older, wealthier friend. This is where the issue of sexual agency emerges. If young people agree to the transaction, and they often do, many such acts are often potentially beyond the scope of the law, depending on their age.

In other words, our existing framework on consent as dividing line between legal and illegal sex acts cannot help. Perhaps if we stopped thinking of this a transaction sex and named it for what it really is, a form of child prostitution, it would be clearer to everybody.

Acknowledge the relationship and the violence

The second issue is when a young person is in an inappropriate relationship. In other words, they think they are a normal girlfriend/ boyfriend but either the perpetrator or those outside the relationship see something different. Quite often, one of the pointers is the age difference between them. But here again, neither the law nor common understandings help us. A 15-year age gap might be problematic when

Forms of sexual violence or exploitation against young women identified by interviewees	
Form of sexual violence or exploitation	**Proportion of sample identifying that form**
Pressure to engage in sexual activity	65%
Distribution of sexual images	50%
Sex in exchange for (perceived) status or protection	50%
Individual perpetrator rape	41%
Sex in exchange for other tangible goods	39%
Multiple perpetrator rape	34%
Young women being used to set up males in rival gangs	31%
Males targeting young women for sexual relationships or sexually assaulting young women as a means of getting at a rival gang	30%
Sexual activity with multiple males	29%
Other sexual assault	23%
Sex in exchange for money	23%
Sexual assault with a weapon	11%
Sex as a means of initiation into the gang	7%

*96 participants were interviewed

those involved are 16 and 31, but not seen as a problem when 60 and 75.

A more important element is the level of power and control exercised by the perpetrator; this is what the exploitation depends on. We already have a good framework to think about this, it is called domestic violence. So rather than dismissing what young people see as a genuine relationship out of hand, using a domestic violence framework would acknowledge the relationship but highlight the abuse.

Focus on race muddies waters

The final area is the one currently receiving most attention, organised networks involving child sexual exploitation. It is at this stage that young people are most likely to begin to see themselves as victims, but some may still not recognise this. Again, this is not a new crime, and the links to international child trafficking should not be overlooked.

However, the current media focus on ethnicity as a key factor is in danger of hiding other perpetrators. White people are in abusive networks too. Focusing on Asian gangs builds on existing Islamaphobia and the notion of child abusers as identifiable monsters rather than the person next door.

What is wrong with our communities?

All these factors focus on the perpetrators of the abuse, rather than the wider context in which these acts take place. Yet it is in this social context that perhaps we need to look for answers. Balancing the line between allowing young people to have some control over their lives and protecting them from abuse is not easy. But if transaction sex and inappropriate relationships are often the gateway to greater forms of abuse, we need to consider why they take place.

Why are the lives of some children and young people so impoverished that they feel the need to swap oral sex for a taxi ride or mobile phone? Perpetrators gain initial power over victims because they make them feel wanted, cared for, and grown up. What is so wrong in our communities that lead to young people being vulnerable to this form of abuse? We ignore this at our peril. If we really want to prevent abuse from taking place, we need to pay as much attention to the lives of all our young people as we do the hunt for those who would abuse them.

11 June 2013

⇨ The above information is reprinted with kind permission from The Conversation. Please visit www.theconversation.com for further information.

Hidden children

Separated children at risk.

Hidden children are migrants under 18-years-old who are separated from their usual carers and are exploited or otherwise mistreated by the people who are responsible for them in the UK. 'Hidden' is intended to refer to the unseen nature of the exploitation, the lack of awareness about these young people and the fact that exploiters deliberately act to keep them and their treatment hidden. Under the 2000 Palermo Protocol, these young people would usually be considered to have been trafficked to the UK to be exploited. Others may not have been brought to the UK to be exploited but later end up living in abusive private fostering arrangements.

Key research findings

Background

Hidden children come from many countries and a wide range of backgrounds. Some enter the UK with or to join family members and some are trafficked clandestinely.

Something that the young people in this research had in common was a lack of influence on the decision made about them.

I thought it was a holiday, I didn't know I was going to stay here. I can't turn around and say to my mum that I don't want to go, because she would just say, do you want to stay here and die? (16-year-old girl who came to the UK aged ten)

I was brought up in a family in which you have to give respect to your elders, and that's defined my whole way of life until now. I thought if I argued with people I'd get in trouble. (African boy exploited through domestic servitude)

If you put yourself into the position of an eight-year-old child and you're told that you're going to do this and this is what you have to say by a grown up that you trust, you follow instruction don't you? (Social work employee of a local authority)

Experience in UK

Once they are in the UK, hidden children may have a range of freedom.

Some children attend school and access healthcare while also being exploited through domestic servitude, forced labour or other abuse.

Some even experience this abuse while in a private fostering arrangement known to social services.

The young people stay in the abusive situations because they don't know that:

⇨ their treatment is illegal

⇨ they will not end up homeless on the streets if they run away

⇨ they will not be immediately deported for disclosing to the authorities

⇨ there are people they can trust to disclose that they have been abused.

Some hidden children who did disclose abuse found frontline workers unwilling to help, disbelieving the seriousness of their situation or unaware of where to refer them for help.

Disclosures, interventions and escapes

Key places for intervening in the abuse of hidden children are in the community, education settings, health settings and faith settings. Any frontline worker or community member can be approached with a disclosure or intervene by recognising signs of exploitation.

Case studies

A 15-year-old boy ran away from an abusive guardian and found a job to pay rent. He attended school during the day and was picked up from school to work in a factory until up to 3am. He was doing his GCSEs and finding it hard to concentrate because of what he was going through. He wanted to do well at his GCSEs, so he told a teacher about his situation. The advisor did not know what his rights were in this case, so took him to a local community advice organisation who said they could not advise him because he did not have settled status. His school advisor then referred him to a refugee charity that supported his asylum application and with being taken into care.

A 12-year-old girl was trafficked for domestic servitude, but after a few months was abandoned on the street by the guardian. A refugee charity worker brought her to an appointment with an immigration solicitor, and the girl disclosed to the solicitor what had happened though she did not want to talk about it.

A teenage girl disclosed to the pastor at her church that she was being emotionally abused by her guardian. The pastor advised that she should pray and try not to make the guardian angry.

A boy ran away from his exploiters and went to an ethnic shop where people spoke his language. Someone in the shop told him about a migrant community group for people from his country, so he went there to ask for help.

Effects of experiences – case studies

One young woman who escaped from her traffickers eight years ago, believes they are looking for her in her home country and will find and recognise her if she is sent home.

One young man in his 20s who has been away from his exploiter for eight years still feels upset when he sees his ex-guardian's car in the street.

One young woman who spent 18 months in domestic labour ran away and was taken into care at age 15. She had not been in school while being exploited, but was put straight into a class that was revising for GCSEs. It upset her that she didn't understand what they were studying. Now she is in the last year of college and is still struggling. The college teachers expect the students to be able to cope on their own, and the migrant students to cope as well as the British-born students.

One boy was thrown out by his abusive guardian and worked illegally to support himself while also attending college. By the time he found out he needed to regularise his status in the UK, he was 18 years old. When he went to the Home Office to apply for asylum, he was put in detention.

Many hidden children will have undergone several types of mistreatment and trauma both before and after coming to the UK. An individual young person may have experienced war and bereavement, a frightening journey to the UK, domestic servitude and sexual exploitation, and the realisation that they were lied to or sold by their guardians/traffickers. Any one or combination of these may be the most traumatising to individual young people.

Additionally, hidden children may experience ambivalent feelings about their families and their exploiters as well as identity issues. Practical difficulties experienced by hidden children include access to essential services such as being taken into care, education, and advice on their immigration status.

Moving on and building a new life

Access to their rights and entitlements and certainty about immigration status are vital for hidden children to be able to move forward after escaping an exploitative situation. Like other separated children, hidden children may experience a spectrum of support based on the resources, thresholds and procedures of their particular Local Authority. If they are over age 16, they may be both more vulnerable to certain types of exploitation and more likely to be granted access to services.

⇨ The above information is reprinted with kind permission from The Children's Society. Please visit www. childrenssociety.org.uk for further information.

© The Children's Society 2014

Illegal adoption: is it human trafficking?

This week, 382 babies were rescued and 1,000 people arrested in a Chinese sting operation against four illegal adoption rings. In January, a Chinese doctor received a suspended death sentence after her conviction for abducting and selling seven babies between November 2011 and July 2013. At least 26 other cases have been linked to this doctor, and several other people are also in criminal detention.

Illegal adoption is especially prevalent in China, as a result of the government's one child policy and a cultural preference for male children. Of course China is not the only country where illegal adoption occurs. A recent Al Jazeera article highlights orphanages in Nepal deceiving parents and putting children with families up for adoption. A US citizen is facing trafficking charges in Haiti this week, a situation reminiscent of the American missionaries accused of removing Haitian children from the country after the 2010 earthquake. All of these children had at least one parent living, and they were subsequently reunited with family. One American was later found guilty, but her sentence was limited to time already served in jail.

Chinese officials, the media and many others consider the abduction of children for illegal adoption to be human trafficking, but debate still surrounds the issue.

The 1993 Hague Convention on the Protection of Children and Co-operation in Respect of Intercountry Adoption establishes common standards and regulations for international adoption, while recognising that these adoptions can lead to child trafficking.

The 2005 *Trafficking in Persons Report (TIP)*, however, disagrees and states that children who have been put up for adoption through illegal means such as abduction or coercion is not considered human trafficking. The TIP report (2005, 21) states:

'The purposes of baby selling and human trafficking are not necessarily the same. Some individuals assume that baby selling for adoption is a form of human trafficking because trafficking and baby selling both involve making a profit by selling another person. However, illegally selling a child for adoption would not constitute trafficking where the child itself is not to be exploited. Baby selling generally results in a situation that is non-exploitative with respect to the child. Trafficking, on the other hand, implies exploitation of the victims. If an adopted child is subjected to coerced labour or sexual exploitation, then it constitutes a case of human trafficking.'

The 2010 TIP report (2010, 8) reiterates this point:

'The kidnapping or unlawful buying/selling of an infant or child for the purpose of offering that child for adoption represents a serious criminal offense, but it is not a form of human trafficking, as it does not necessarily involve the use of force, fraud, or coercion to compel services from a person. As stated in the travaux preparatoires of the Palermo Protocol, only "where illegal adoption amounts to a practice similar to slavery ... it will also fall within the scope of the Protocol." '

Thus, according to the US State Department, if a child is not exploited post-adoption, the adoption act might be illegal, but it is not considered trafficking. This is because the US Trafficking Victims Protection Act follows the UN Protocols on Trafficking in Persons and the Sale of Children in its definition on trafficking.

Even though the US doesn't recognise trafficking of children for adoption purposes, several countries do and have included illegal adoptions in their anti-trafficking legislation. China is an example, as are Sri Lanka, Liberia, Vietnam, Guatemala, Nicaragua, Venezuela and Costa Rica. According to various TIP reports (2010, 122) these countries include illegal adoptions in legislation which 'does not fall within the international definition of human trafficking'.

In Child Trafficking and Australia's Intercountry Adoption System, Siobhan Clair (2012, 13) notes that: 'despite the broad international condemnation of child trafficking, a complete and authoritative legal definition remains difficult to establish, especially in the context of inter country adoption', but she also notes that 'the Australian Government appears to accept that child trafficking may occur through the adoption system, even where no exploitation is present'.

David Smolin (2004, 302) writes in *Intercountry Adoption as Child Trafficking* that international law 'has been reluctant to label all sales of children as prohibited forms of child trafficking and has failed to demand penal sanctions for all abusive adoption practices'; however, 'the law has been moving in the direction of clearly labelling certain abusive adoption practices as prohibited forms of child trafficking or sale of children'.

UNICEF, for its part, considers illegal adoption as child trafficking. In UNICEF's 2009 report *Child Trafficking in East and South-East Asia: Reversing the Trend* (2009, 32), adoption is listed as one of the reasons why children are trafficked in the region, but UNICEF notes that 'existing literature in the region overwhelmingly concentrates on trafficking for sexual exploitation, while systematic research on more diverse forms, such as trafficking of children for adoption and marriage, is lacking'. UNICEF (2009, 84) also considers illegal adoption exploitation when it recommends the criminalisation of 'all forms of exploitation, including but not limited to: sexual abuse and sexual exploitation, domestic servitude, debt bondage, involvement in armed conflict, organ/tissue removal and transport, illegal adoption and forced marriage'. This directly contradicts what the US asserts in the 2005 and 2010 TIP reports (cited above) that illegal adoption is not exploitation if it does not lead to forced labour or sexual exploitation.

And while international law does not specifically label illegal adoption human trafficking, the UNODC *Global Report on Trafficking in Persons* (2012, 12) does: 'Trafficking for purposes not specifically mentioned in the Trafficking in Persons Protocol, including begging, forced marriages, illegal adoption, participation in armed combat and the commission of crime (usually petty crime/street crime) accounted for six per cent of the total number of detected cases in 2010,' and the UNODC (2012, 37) reports that: 'cases of trafficking for the purposes of illegal adoption have been detected in 15 countries'.

The UN acknowledges that trafficking of children for illegal adoption is not in the Trafficking in Persons Protocol, but it still considers the practice of obtaining children – like the 382 Chinese babies rescued this week – through abduction, coercion, or other illegal means to be child trafficking.

This begs the question, why doesn't the US?

2 March 2014

⇨ The above information is reprinted with kind permission from Human Trafficking Indicators. Please visit www.humantraffickingindicators.org for further information.

It happens here

Equipping the United Kingdom to fight modern slavery.

Modern slavery in the UK

Modern slavery exists in the UK and destroys lives. It manifests in an appallingly wide range of forms. Adults and children – UK nationals and those from abroad – are exploited in the sex industry, through forced labour, domestic servitude in the home, and forced criminal activity. The CSJ has gathered evidence on numerous cases of exploitation in factories, fields, construction sites, brothels and houses.

Our research shows that a large proportion of cases are never recognised or reported, and do not appear in any statistics or measures of the size of the problem. There is no consistent grip on the numbers; agencies charged with such responsibility are groping in the dark for a sense of scale. The figures used below reflect the small number of cases known about, but are a pale reflection of the true size of the problem.

Definition

Modern slavery

Human trafficking

1. Recruitment, transportation, transfer, harbouring or receipt of persons;

2. By means of threat or use of force or other forms of coercion, of abduction, of fraud, of deception, of the abuse of power or of a position of vulnerability or of the giving or receiving of payments or benefits to achieve the consent of a person having control over another person (where a child is involved, the above means are irrelevant);

3. For the purposes of exploitation, which shall include (non-exhaustive):

a. Prostitution;

b. Other sexual exploitation;

c. Forced labour;

d. Slavery (or similar);

e. Servitude, etc.;

f. Removal of organs.

Slavery

The status or condition of a person over whom any or all of the powers attaching to the right of ownership are exercised (129 Convention; approved in defining art 4 ECHR: Siladin v France (ECHR, 2005)).

Servitude

An obligation to provide one's services that is imposed by the use of coercion, and is to be linked with the concept of 'slavery' described above (Siladin v France, ECHR (2005)).

Forced labour

All work or service which is exacted from any person under the menace of any penalty and for which the said person has not offered himself voluntarily.

March 2013

⇨ The above information is reprinted with kind permission from The Centre for Social Justice. Please visit www.centreforsocialjustice.org.uk for further information.

Jess and Hannah

Jess and Hannah, two UK-born school children, met a small group of young men who began to flatter and treat them, and convince the girls that they were in love. Before long, the girls began to be pressured and forced into performing sexual acts on the young men and their older friends. One weekend the girls were driven to a flat and told that they must have sex with whoever arrived at the property. Jess was menstruating, and so was forced to sit outside the room. Hannah had no option and, over the weekend, was raped by 90 men. Both of these girls were victims of modern slavery within the UK.[1]

1 Names have been changed

Key facts

- It's estimated that about 150,000,000 children (5–14-years-old) are involved in child labour worldwide. If we consider all young people who are under 18, some estimates are as high as 246 million. Of these, nearly 70% work in hazardous conditions. (page 2)

- Regional estimates indicate that the largest number of child workers in the five to 14 age group are in the Asia and Pacific region where 127.3 million children work. (page 2)

- In sub-Saharan Africa there is an estimated 48 million child workers – that's almost one child in three below the age of 15 who is economically active. (page 3)

- It is estimated that 60% child labourers work in agriculture, 26% in services and 7% in industry, with the remainder in undefined work. (page 3)

- India officially produces about 15,000 tonnes of crude and scrap mica a year... yet it exported more than 130,000 tonnes – more than eight times the official production figure – in 2011–12. (page 7)

- Maplecroft's analysis indicates that child labour risks are also increasing in sub-Saharan Africa, which hosts 43 (over 50%) of the 'extreme risk' countries in the Child Labour Index. (page 11)

- In September 2013, the International Labour Organization (ILO) estimated that the rate of 5–17-year-olds engaged in child labour has decreased globally from 13.6 per cent in 2008 to 10.6 per cent in 2012. The number of children involved in the worst forms of child labour has also decreased from 115 million to 85 million during this time. (page 11)

- There are estimated to be between 100 million and 150 million street children in the world, and this number is growing. Of those some 5–10% have run away from or been abandoned by their families. (page 14)

- Under international law, the participation of children under 18 in armed conflict is generally prohibited. (page 14)

- Children in the poorest households are three times more likely to have a mental illness than children in the best off households. (page 18)

- Deaths from measles among children under five years of age fell from 482,000 in 2000 to 86,000 in 2012, thanks in large part to immunisation coverage, which increased from 16 per cent in 1980 to 84 per cent in 2012. (page 19)

- The number of out-of-school children of primary school age increased in sub-Saharan Africa to 30 million in 2011 from 29 million in 2008, with Nigeria housing a third of all these children – an estimated 10.5 million out-of-school children. (page 22)

- In Cambodia, a working child is 17% less likely to enter school at the official age and thus runs a higher risk of dropout. (page 23)

- There are more than 1,700 teenagers in the armed forces below voting age. The vast majority of 16- and 17-year-olds are in the Army, according to the 2014 annual personnel report. (page 27)

- Research has shown that 16-year-old recruits are much more likely than adults to suffer bullying and harassment, to develop serious mental health problems, to be injured in training, and to be killed once they reach deployable age. (page 27)

- One in three girls in the developing world will be married by their eighteenth birthday. If nothing is done to stop current trends, more than 140 million girls will be married as children by 2020. That's 14 million every year or nearly 39,000 girls married every day. (page 28)

- More than 140 million girls will become child brides by 2020, if current rates of child marriage continue. (page 29)

- Every year, nearly 13.7 million 15- to 19-year-old girls in the developing world give birth while married. Complications in pregnancy and childbirth are the leading cause of mortality for girls aged 15 to 19 in developing countries. (page 29)

- More than 140 million girls will become child brides by 2020, if current rates of child marriage continue. (page 29)

- 39,000 girls under 18 are married every day. (page 30)

- A UK-wide survey estimated that in 2009-2010, there were over 3,000 young people accessing services because they had been affected by sexual exploitation. (page 32)

Boycott

A form of activism in which consumers refuse to buy a product or use a service to protest against unethical practices by the manufacturer/provider.

Child exploitation

Child exploitation is a broad term which includes forced or dangerous labour, child trafficking and child prostitution. The term is used to refer to situations where children are abused – physically, verbally or sexually – or when they are submitted to unsatisfactory conditions as part of their forced or voluntary employment.

Child labour

There is no universally-accepted definition of child labour. However, it might generally be said to be work for children that harms or exploits them in some way (physically, mentally, morally or by blocking access to education). According to the International Labour Organization, more than 168 million children worldwide are still in child labour and 85 million at least are subject to its worst forms (are in hazardous work).

Child marriage

Where children, often before they have reached puberty, are given to be married – often to a person many years older.

Child soldiers

A child soldier is a person under the age of 18 associated with an armed force or group, who has been recruited or used by an armed group in any capacity. This includes children, both boys and girls, used as fighters, cooks, porters, spies, domestic servants or for sexual purposes. It does not only refer to a child who is taking, or has taken, a direct part in hostilities. Child soldiers may be volunteers, or they may have been abducted, forced or coerced into their position by the armed group with which they are associated.

Child trafficking

'Trafficking' is not the same as 'people smuggling', where immigrants and asylum seekers pay people to help them enter another country illegally. Victims of trafficking are coerced or deceived by the person arranging their relocation. On arrival in the country of destination, a trafficked child is denied their human rights and forced into exploitation by the trafficker or person into whose control they are delivered.

Children's rights

The Convention on the Rights of the Child (CRC) is a human rights treaty which has changed the way that children are viewed and treated since it was established in 1989. The treat sets out the civil, political, economic, social, health and cultural rights of children.

Commercial sexual exploitation of children

The Declaration and Agenda for Action against Commercial Sexual Exploitation of Children defines this as 'a fundamental violation of children's rights. It comprises sexual abuse by the adult and remuneration in cash or kind to the child or a third person or persons. The child is treated as a sexual object and a commercial object. The commercial sexual exploitation of children constitutes a form of coercion and violence against children, and amounts to forced labour and a contemporary form of slavery'. Commercial sexual exploitation of children may take the form of child abuse through the prostitution of children; using children to create images of child sex abuse (child 'pornography'); providing children to visitors from overseas for the purpose of sexual abuse (child sex tourism), and child marriage where a child is used for sexual purposes in exchange for goods or services. Children who are sexually exploited in these ways may have been trafficked from another country for that purpose.

DDR

This abbreviation stands for Disarmament, Demobilisation and Reintegration. It refers to the programmes which are in place in some regions to help rehabilitate child soldiers: they are rescued from the armed groups they are associated with, helped to deal with psychological damage arising from their traumatic experiences and hopefully are then able to be reintegrated into their communities.

Debt bondage

Also called bonded labour, this means that an individual is forced to pay off a debt by working for the person to whom they owe money. Where someone is made to work for little or no pay, or for a far longer period than it would take to pay their debt, this can be seen as a form of modern-day slavery. In some situations, whole families, including children, can be held in bonded labour, or children can be forced to work on behalf of another family member who owes money.

Domestic labour

Work which takes place in the home: for example, minding children, cooking, cleaning.

Illegal adoption

The 2010 Trafficking in Persons Report defines illegal adoption as 'The kidnapping or unlawful buying/selling of an infant or child for the purpose of offering that child for adoption'. This is a serious criminal offense, but it is technically not a form of human trafficking because it does not necessarily involve the use of force, fraud or coercion to compel services from a person. Illegal adoption is especially prevalent in China, as a result of the government's one child policy and a cultural preference for male children.

Sweatshop

A hazardous or exploitative working environment, where employees may work long hours for very low pay. Employers often violate legal requirements regarding workers' rights, such as minimum pay regulations.

Assignments

Brainstorming

⇨ In small groups, discuss what you know about child labour and exploitation. Consider the following points:

- What is child labour?

- What is child exploitation?

- Is there a difference between child labour and child work?

- What are child soldiers?

- What is the Convention on the Rights of the Child (CRC)?

Research

⇨ Do some research about child soldiers. Make some notes and feedback to your class.

⇨ Research 'modern slavery' and write a report on your findings.

⇨ Choose a table from this book, such as the one on page 23, and create a graph that illustrates its information.

⇨ Research illegal adoption and write an article or blog post exploring your findings.

Design

⇨ Design a poster that will raise awareness of child marriage.

⇨ Choose one of the articles in this book and create an illustration to highlight the key themes/message of your chosen article.

⇨ Design a leaflet that explains child labour. Try to include some maps and statistics, as well as images or drawings.

⇨ Design a website that will give parents information about child sexual exploitation. Think about the kind of information they might need and give your site a name and logo.

Oral

⇨ 'Child labour is a tragic but necessary economic evil which enables emerging economies to progress and the very poorest to survive.' Debate this motion as a class, with one group arguing in favour and the other against.

⇨ Look at Maplecroft's Child Labour Index 2014 map on page 10. Choose one of the 'extreme risk' countries and research child labour in that country. Create a five-minute presentation that explores your findings and share with your class. You could include images, videos, maps and statistics to engage your audience.

⇨ As a class, discuss whether you believe boys should be allowed to wear skirts to school. Read the article *Let boys wear skirts to school, says children adviser Tam Baille* (page 16) to help inform your opinions.

Reading/writing

⇨ Find out about the use of child labour in the UK during a historical period of your choosing. What kinds of work were children expected to do? What hazards existed for working children? How much would they have been paid? Write an article exploring your findings.

⇨ Read *Oliver Twist* by Charles Dickens and write a review, focusing on the type of world Oliver inhabits and its attitude to children and childhood.

⇨ Imagine you work for a charity which campaigns against child marriage in the UK. Write a blog-post for your charity's website explaining the issues surrounding child marriage and your feelings about the issue.

⇨ Write a one-paragraph definition of child labour.

⇨ Read the article *How does child labour prevent literacy?* (page 2) and write a summary for your school newspaper.

⇨ Write a diary entry from the perspective of a child worker. What kind of work do you do? What do you think your future will be like? How do you feel about your work?

Acknowledgements

The publisher is grateful for permission to reproduce the material in this book. While every care has been taken to trace and acknowledge copyright, the publisher tenders its apology for any accidental infringement or where copyright has proved untraceable. The publisher would be pleased to come to a suitable arrangement in any such case with the rightful owner.

Images

All images courtesy of iStock, except page 15: Morguefile and page 21 © Jackie Staines.

Illustrations

Don Hatcher: pages 8 & 11. Simon Kneebone: pages 20 & 24. Angelo Madrid: pages 4 & 37.

Additional acknowledgements

Editorial on behalf of Independence Educational Publishers by Cara Acred.

With thanks to the Independence team: Mary Chapman, Sandra Dennis, Christina Hughes, Jackie Staines and Jan Sunderland.

Cara Acred

Cambridge

September 2014